The phenomenological features of M
embodiment have today received ext‹
biological and neuroscientific researcl
and distills the pivotal insights of the
reading for every architect who might ponder how people actually
perceive their designed environments.

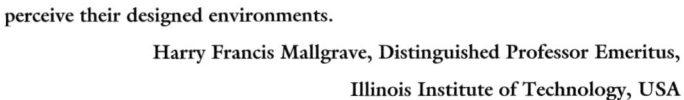

                Harry Francis Mallgrave, Distinguished Professor Emeritus,
                                            Illinois Institute of Technology, USA

MERLEAU-PONTY FOR ARCHITECTS

The philosophy of Maurice Merleau-Ponty (1908–1961) has influenced the design work of architects as diverse as Steven Holl and Peter Zumthor, as well as informing renowned schools of architectural theory, notably those around Dalibor Vesely at Cambridge, UK; Kenneth Frampton, David Leatherbarrow and Alberto Pérez-Gómez in North America; and Juhani Pallasmaa in Finland. Merleau-Ponty suggested that the value of people's experience of the world, gained through their immediate bodily engagement with it, remains greater than the value of understanding gleaned through abstract mathematical, scientific or technological systems.

This book summarizes what Merleau-Ponty's philosophy has to offer specifically for architects. It locates architectural thinking in the context of his work, placing it in relation to themes such as space, movement, materiality and creativity. It introduces key texts, helps decode difficult terms and provides quick reference for further reading.

**Jonathan Hale** is Associate Professor and Reader in Architectural Theory at the University of Nottingham, UK.

# Thinkers for Architects

**Series Editor: Adam Sharr, Newcastle University, UK**

**Editorial Board**

Jonathan A. Hale, University of Nottingham, UK
Hilde Heynen, KU Leuven, Netherlands
David Leatherbarrow, University of Pennsylvania, USA

Architects have often looked to philosophers and theorists from beyond the discipline for design inspiration or in search of a critical framework for practice. This original series offers quick, clear introductions to key thinkers who have written about architecture and whose work can yield insights for designers.

> 'Each unintimidatingly slim book makes sense of the subjects' complex theories.'
>
> **Building Design**

> '... a valuable addition to any studio space or computer lab.'
>
> **Architectural Record**

> '... a creditable attempt to present their subjects in a useful way.'
>
> **Architectural Review**

**Foucault for Architects**
Gordana Fontana-Giusti

**Virilio for Architects**
John Armitage

**Goodman for Architects**
Remei Capdevila-Werning

**Baudrillard for Architects**
Francesco Proto

**Lefebvre for Architects**
Nathaniel Coleman

**Merleau-Ponty for Architects**
Jonathan Hale

THINKERS FOR ARCHITECTS

# Merleau-Ponty

for

Architects

Jonathan Hale

Routledge
Taylor & Francis Group
LONDON AND NEW YORK

First published 2017
by Routledge
2 Park Square, Milton Park, Abingdon, Oxon OX14 4RN

and by Routledge
711 Third Avenue, New York, NY 10017

*Routledge is an imprint of the Taylor & Francis Group, an informa business*

© 2017 Jonathan Hale

The right of Jonathan Hale to be identified as author of this work has been asserted by him in accordance with sections 77 and 78 of the Copyright, Designs and Patents Act 1988.

All rights reserved. No part of this book may be reprinted or reproduced or utilised in any form or by any electronic, mechanical, or other means, now known or hereafter invented, including photocopying and recording, or in any information storage or retrieval system, without permission in writing from the publishers.

*Trademark notice:* Product or corporate names may be trademarks or registered trademarks, and are used only for identification and explanation without intent to infringe.

*British Library Cataloguing-in-Publication Data*
A catalogue record for this book is available from the British Library

*Library of Congress Cataloging-in-Publication Data*
Names: Hale, Jonathan A., author.
Title: Merleau-Ponty for architects / Jonathan Hale.
Description: New York : Routledge, 2016. | Includes bibliographical references and index.
Identifiers: LCCN 2016002697 | ISBN 9780415480710 (hardback : alk. paper) | ISBN 9780415480727 (pbk. : alk. paper) | ISBN 9781315645438 (ebook)
Subjects: LCSH: Merleau-Ponty, Maurice, 1908-1961. | Architecture--Philosophy.
Classification: LCC B2430.M3764 H34 2016 | DDC 194--dc23
LC record available at http://lccn.loc.gov/2016002697

ISBN: 978-0-415-48071-0 (hbk)
ISBN: 978-0-415-48072-7 (pbk)
ISBN: 978-1-315-64543-8 (ebk)

Typeset in Frutiger
by Saxon Graphics Ltd, Derby

Printed and bound in Great Britain by
TJ International Ltd, Padstow, Cornwall

For Jocelyn

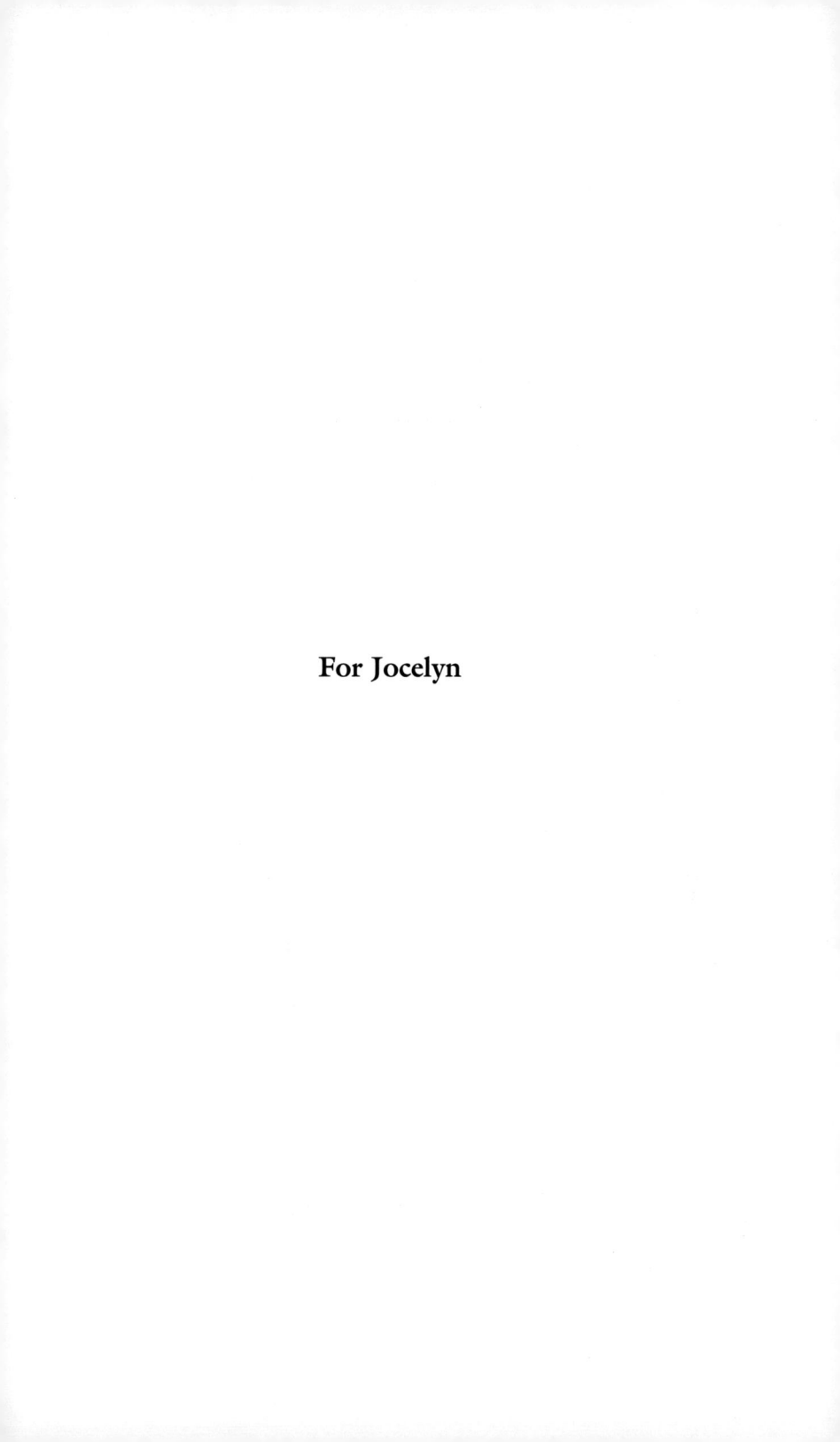

# Contents

Series editor's preface     xi
Illustration credits     xiii
Acknowledgements     xv

1. Introduction     1

   Phenomenology and architecture   3
   Merleau-Ponty and architecture   5
   Who was Maurice Merleau-Ponty?   7

2. Embodied space: it's not what you think     9

   Body schemas   13
   Motor cognition   16
   Place and memory   20
   From Bauhaus to Koolhaas   22
   The social body   23
   From the extended body to the extended mind   27

3. Expressive form: since feeling is first     38

   Learning to see   39
   The thickness of time and the depth of space   43
   The bodily form of things   48
   Architecture of empathy   54

4. Tectonics and materials: the flesh of the world — 62

   Dualism redoubled? 62
   The reversibility of the flesh 66
   Ideas and things 71
   Reversible architecture 75
   Living materiality and environmental ethics 82

5. Creativity and innovation: from *spoken* to *speaking* speech — 87

   Seeing through painting 87
   The language of experience 90
   Between spontaneity and repetition 96
   Reverting to type 98
   Material methods 100
   Reuse and reinterpretation 107

6. 'There is nothing outside embodiment' — 112

   Further reading — 116
   Bibliography — 118
   Index — 141

# Series editor's preface

**Adam Sharr**

Architects have often looked to thinkers in philosophy and theory for design ideas, or in search of a critical framework for practice. Yet architects and students of architecture can struggle to navigate thinkers' writings. It can be daunting to approach original texts with little appreciation of their contexts. And existing introductions seldom explore a thinker's architectural material in any detail. This original series offers clear, quick and accurate introductions to key thinkers who have written about architecture. Each book summarizes what a thinker has to offer for architects. It locates their architectural thinking in the body of their work, introduces significant books and essays, helps decode terms and provides quick reference for further reading. If you find philosophical and theoretical writing about architecture difficult, or just don't know where to begin, this series will be indispensable.

Books in the *Thinkers for Architects* series come out of architecture. They pursue architectural modes of understanding, aiming to introduce a thinker to an architectural audience. Each thinker has a unique and distinctive ethos, and the structure of each book derives from the character at its focus. The thinkers explored are prodigious writers and any short introduction can only address a fraction of their work. Each author – an architect or an architectural critic – has focused on a selection of a thinker's writings which they judge most relevant to designers and interpreters of architecture. Inevitably, much will be left out. These books will be the first point of reference, rather than the last word, about a particular thinker for architects. It is hoped that they will encourage you to read further, offering an incentive to delve deeper into the original writings of a particular thinker.

The *Thinkers for Architects* series has proved highly successful, expanding to fourteen volumes dealing with familiar cultural figures whose writings have influenced architectural designers, critics and commentators in distinctive and important ways. Books explore the work of: Gilles Deleuze and Felix Guattari; Martin Heidegger; Luce Irigaray; Homi Bhabha; Pierre Bourdieu; Walter Benjamin; Jacques Derrida; Hans-Georg Gadamer, Michael Foucault, Nelson Goodman, Henri Lefebvre, Paul Virilio, Jean Baudrillard and now Maurice Merleau-Ponty. Future volumes are projected, addressing the work of Jacques Lacan and Immanuel Kant. The series continues to expand, addressing an increasingly rich diversity of thinkers who have something to say to architects.

**Adam Sharr** is Professor of Architecture at Newcastle University, Principal of Adam Sharr Architects and Editor-in-Chief of *arq: Architectural Research Quarterly*, a Cambridge University Press international architecture journal. His books published by Routledge include *Heidegger for Architects* and *Reading Architecture and Culture*.

# Illustration credits

1. Introduction

    1. Maurice Merleau-Ponty (1908–61). © www.topfoto.co.uk

2. Embodied space: it's not what you think

    2. Stelarc – THIRD HAND, Tokyo, Yokohama, Nagoya 1980. Photo: Toshifumi Ike. © Stelarc / T. Ike

3. Expressive form: since feeling is first

    3. O'Donnell + Tuomey Architects, Lewis Glucksman Gallery, Cork, 2004. Photo: Jonathan Hale

4. Tectonics and materials: the flesh of the world

    4. Richard Long, *A Line Made By Walking*, 1967. © Richard Long. All Rights Reserved, DACS 2015. Photo: Richard Long
    5. Caruso St John Architects, New Art Gallery, Walsall, 2000. Photo: Jonathan Hale
    6. Caruso St John Architects, New Art Gallery, Walsall. Photo: Jonathan Hale
    7. Caruso St John Architects, New Art Gallery, Walsall; second-floor landing. Photo: Jonathan Hale

# Acknowledgements

I must thank the University of Nottingham for a semester of study-leave in 2009, when I foolishly promised to finish the book by sometime around the end of July. Six years, and several draft versions later, I now have a few more debts to acknowledge. A second short period of leave in the spring of 2013 allowed me to take up a visiting professorship at Carleton University in Ottawa, where the generous hospitality of the Azrieli School of Architecture (especially its – sadly now, late – Director Marco Frascari, and also Roger Connah) provided a stimulating environment to test out ideas.

I am grateful to the series editor Adam Sharr for setting up *Thinkers for Architects*, and to everyone in the Architecture department at Routledge, especially Fran Ford and Georgina Johnson-Cook, for their confidence and their patience. Latterly, I have also benefitted greatly from the good-natured chivvying of Grace Harrison, which finally got me to commit to a deadline. Valuable help with the early research was provided by my former Ph.D. student Xiao Jing, who has since completed a post-doc in the time it has taken to write the book. I have also drawn support from two research groups at Nottingham: *Science Technology and Culture,* run by the inspirational Chris Johnson in the Department of French; and the *Sense of Space* group, based in the Department of Philosophy. The latter began as a joint venture with Komarine Romdenh-Romluc, who has since joined the University of Sheffield, and who also gave some valuable detailed comments on the final draft of the manuscript. Stephen Walker and Harry Francis Mallgrave also offered extremely useful input. I must also thank the guest speakers at various *Sense of Space* events for providing vital moments of inspiration and insight into Merleau-Ponty's work: Thomas Baldwin, Rachel McCann, David Morris and Joel Smith.

Lastly, a special thanks must go to my good friend Terrance Galvin who first pointed me towards the work of Merleau-Ponty – if I remember rightly, in our first week as graduate students at the University of Pennsylvania, in the *'salle des pas perdus'* that is the great Furness Library.

Maurice Merleau-Ponty (1908–61).

CHAPTER 1

# Introduction

The French philosopher Maurice Merleau-Ponty (1908–61) never wrote a book about architecture, not even a chapter or an essay. In fact, despite his frequent references to the everyday situations of 'lived experience', nowhere in his work is there any kind of systematic treatment of buildings, spaces or cities. Therefore, one is clearly entitled to ask at this point: what is there in Merleau-Ponty for architects?

To begin with, he did produce a powerful argument for what he sometimes called the 'primacy of perception'; the idea that perception as an act of the whole body is central to our experience and understanding of the world. Merleau-Ponty's philosophy, building on the early twentieth-century tradition of phenomenology, established by the German philosopher Edmund Husserl and his student Martin Heidegger, focused on the central fact that we are, as human beings, inescapably embodied entities. For Merleau-Ponty, therefore, even more so than for his two illustrious predecessors, the body serves as our first means of access to the world: in other words, before we can even begin to philosophize, we first have to come to terms with the embodied reality of our 'concrete situation'. He also described how, through our constantly evolving repertoire of bodily skills and patterns of behaviour, we learn to 'come to grips' with this world through a process of exploration and discovery. Our initial understanding of a space is based on its practical possibilities – we grasp it as a structured arena for action, inviting us to use it in a particular way. This idea of experience as an ongoing interplay between perception and action has vital implications for how we think about space in architecture today, and more importantly, for how we set about designing places that people find engaging, stimulating and meaningful.

Another reason for architects to look more carefully at Merleau-Ponty's work is that he did write several lengthy and significant articles on other forms of creative expression, most notably on painting and literature. More recently, these essays have been collected and republished as *The Merleau-Ponty Aesthetics Reader* (Johnson and Smith 1993), suggesting that there is plenty here to interest people well beyond the confines of philosophy. More important for architects is Merleau-Ponty's lifelong study of what he called the 'phenomenology of perception': the typically taken-for-granted miracle of everyday experience that results from the ongoing interactions of brain, body and world. Through a persistent and often inspiring evocation of what he referred to as the body's 'primordial encounter' with the everyday world, he described how sense is actually inherent in bodily experience, and how the body acts as the vital pivot between the inner world of the individual and the outer world of social and cultural forces.

One of the commonly repeated misconceptions in many architectural accounts is that phenomenology appears to support the traditional notion of the individual self as an isolated rational 'subject', the idea being that the individual is some kind of sovereign creator of meaning, able to magically constitute the world independently as a product of conscious thought (Hensel et al. 2009: 145). One of the key aims of this book is to set out a radically alternative view, to suggest that Merleau-Ponty should, in fact, be seen as a 'proto-posthumanist' thinker: someone who believes in a fluid definition of the individual self, or subject, as both dependent on and inseparable from its natural and cultural surroundings. Merleau-Ponty also supports the idea of the *Umwelt*, developed by the biologist Jakob von Uexküll, which shows how all organisms effectively 'produce' their own environment by selecting just those features of the world with which they are equipped to interact. In other words, it is our ability to perceive a particular quality (the colour green, for example) that allows it to 'show up' as a characteristic of 'our' particular world. It is here, at the point of contact between bodily behaviour and environmental opportunity, that an organism begins to make sense of its existence and ultimately – and likewise over an evolutionary timescale – to emerge into a state of consciousness (Merleau-Ponty 2003: 167; 1983: 159). Merleau-Ponty described this mutual interdependence between the self and its surroundings by saying that 'the world is inseparable from the subject, but a subject who is nothing but a project of the world' (Merleau-Ponty 2012: 454).

<u>Merleau-Ponty should, in fact, be seen as a 'proto-posthumanist' thinker: someone who believes in a fluid definition of the individual self, both dependent on and inseparable from its surroundings.</u>

### Phenomenology and architecture

A further reason for the continued architectural relevance of Merleau-Ponty's work is the key contribution it made to the growth and influence of the larger phenomenological 'movement'. As one of the major schools of twentieth-century philosophy, phenomenology has had a significant impact in architecture and many other fields concerned with the relations between intellectual ideas and material things. Inaugurated by the German philosopher Edmund Husserl in 1900, with the publication of his *Logical Investigations*, phenomenology in its modern form set out to challenge some of the most basic principles in the history of Western philosophy, including the long-standing split between the mind and the body that had been prevalent since the time of Plato. This effort was even more evident in the work of Husserl's most illustrious student, Martin Heidegger, whose ideas drew almost as much from the few surviving fragments of so-called Pre-Socratic philosophy as they did from the 2,000 years of writing that came after. While Husserl's own writings have not been as directly influential in architecture, Heidegger's ideas have been taken up by a number of architectural historians, theorists and designers (Sharr 2007).

Much of the most important work in phenomenology was produced in the 1940s and 1950s, but it took until the 1960s before these ideas had a real impact in architecture, particularly in the English-speaking world. This was partly due to the time lag between original publication and translation; two of the most significant single works, Heidegger's *Being and Time* and Merleau-Ponty's *Phenomenology of Perception* both first appeared in English only in 1962. An important early link between phenomenology and architectural theory came through the work of Christian Norberg-Schulz, although his earliest writings, such as the book *Intentions in Architecture* (Norberg-Schulz 1966), were, as with Merleau-Ponty's early work, more strongly influenced by Gestalt psychology. This is a school of thought developed in the early 1900s, based on the idea that we perceive the world only insofar as it appears to us immediately in 'structured wholes' or meaningful patterns, as opposed to random sequences of incoming sensory 'data', which the perceiving subject then has to 'decode' and interpret. Norberg-Schulz's later work borrowed more directly from Heidegger, particularly his 1951 essay 'Building Dwelling Thinking', which inspired the idea of the 'spirit of place' as emerging gradually through the dynamic and active processes of dwelling in a particular environment (Norberg-Schulz 1985). By accepting the limited natural resources provided by the site and working in harmony with the local climate and traditional building patterns, it was claimed that this spirit could be preserved and reinterpreted, and thus extended into the future.

In this emphasis on tradition in both dwelling patterns and technologies, the phenomenological approach in architecture soon became associated with conservatism and nostalgia. On the other hand, a number of more recent architectural writers such as Kenneth Frampton and Juhani Pallasmaa have also tried to emphasize the potentially liberating power of a return to the fundamental principles of form, space and materiality. These possibilities are perhaps best evidenced in the buildings of phenomenologically inspired designers such as Peter Zumthor and Steven Holl and also the early work of the Swiss practice Herzog and de Meuron. By focusing on the central role of the moving body in the perception of architectural space, the sensory qualities of light, sound, temperature and materiality can be thought of in Merleau-Ponty's terms as a kind of 'primordial language', often only experienced unconsciously by building users as part of the background to their everyday activities.

Ultimately, phenomenology in architecture is less of a design method and more a form of discourse, offering a powerful way of describing, discussing and 'deciding about' architecture, from the perspective of our lived experience as embodied building users. It provides a set of tools to help us both design and dwell more rewardingly within our buildings, by heightening our awareness of the teeming richness of the world that is constantly unfolding around us. As Merleau-Ponty himself suggests, phenomenology as a 'way of seeing' could be compared with poetry and painting, as he considers it

> as painstaking as the works of Balzac, Proust, Valéry, or Cézanne – through the same kind of attention and wonder, the same demand for awareness, the same will to grasp the sense of the world or of history in its nascent state.
> (Merleau-Ponty 2012: lxxxv)

Ultimately, phenomenology in architecture is less of a design method and more a form of discourse, offering a powerful way of describing, discussing and deciding.

### Merleau-Ponty and architecture

The major implications of Merleau-Ponty's ideas for architects can be described under the broad headings of Ethics and Aesthetics, and both of these areas will be addressed in detail in the four main chapters to follow. On the one hand, his famously complex concept of 'flesh' suggests an underlying continuity between the body and the world, providing a powerful philosophical grounding for what we might call an 'ethical ecology' – a reminder that we should all be much more mindful of our ultimate dependence on our surroundings. On the other hand, his work also offers a way of addressing our often unconscious aesthetic preferences, by showing how our perception of the world around us necessarily begins with a process of bodily engagement, before it can be processed in intellectual terms and chopped up into concepts. His profound meditation on the primacy of embodied perception suggests that the body serves ultimately as both a framework and a model for everything we can come to know about ourselves and the world.

There has also been a recent revival of interest in Merleau-Ponty's work on embodied perception across a number of related research areas, including philosophy of mind, cognitive science, artificial intelligence and neuroscience, where the central role of the body has now become well established (Gibbs 2005; Clark 2008; Clarke and Hansen 2009; Shapiro 2011). I have tried to give a sense of this burgeoning interest by drawing on literature from across a range of fields, especially where new evidence is helping to refine and substantiate claims that were perhaps only vaguely formulated by Merleau-Ponty himself. My other aim is to show the relevance of his work across a broader range of architectural issues, beyond the more obvious application to questions of materiality and sensory experience.

Of course, gaps remain in Merleau-Ponty's account of embodiment: the role of gender being perhaps the most significant, despite his occasional reference to the writing of his friend Simone de Beauvoir. His work certainly allows room to incorporate sexual difference, as later writers like Iris Marion Young and Elizabeth Grosz have already convincingly shown (Young 1980; Grosz 1994; Olkowski and Weiss 2006). What they highlight is the potential in Merleau-Ponty's approach to account for the implications of different forms of embodiment, beyond the simple binary opposition of male and female: 'there is a particular style of bodily comportment that is typical of feminine existence, and this style consists of particular modalities of the structures and conditions of the body's existence in the world' (Young 1980: 141).

> ... [there is] the potential in Merleau-Ponty's approach to account for the implications of different forms of embodiment, beyond the simple binary opposition of male and female.

As it is almost impossible to present Merleau-Ponty's ideas in any kind of straightforward linear sequence, this book is organized according to broad architectural themes, following a cyclical and iterative pattern. Each chapter therefore deals in different ways with many of the same ideas. Building on the brief outline provided in this introduction, later chapters will attempt to flesh out a progressively more detailed picture. Chapters 2, 3 and 4 develop the key elements of Merleau-Ponty's work in relation to questions of space, form and materiality in architecture, while Chapter 5 highlights the more radical and creative implications for design of what he described as the gradual emergence of reason out of bodily experience.

## Who was Maurice Merleau-Ponty?

Maurice Merleau-Ponty was born on 14 March 1908, in Rochefort-sur-Mer, on the west coast of France. Following his father's death in 1913 he was raised as a Catholic in Paris by his mother, along with his brother and sister. After enjoying what he later described as a prolonged and exceptionally happy childhood, his career followed the typical path of a high-flying French academic. After sitting the entrance exams a year early, he studied philosophy at the École Normale Supérieure in Paris from 1926 to 1930, making friends with future stars of the post-war intellectual scene such as Jean-Paul Sartre and Simone de Beauvoir, with whom he later founded the still-influential literary–political journal *Les Temps Modernes*. From 1933–34, while teaching philosophy at a *lycée* (sixth-form college) in Beauvais, he produced his first pieces of scholarly research on the nature of perception, influenced by the latest developments in both phenomenology and Gestalt psychology. After returning to the École Normale as a junior lecturer in 1935, he submitted his Ph.D. 'minor thesis', which was later published as a book called *The Structure of Behavior* (1942). In the meantime he had also served for twelve months as a lieutenant in the French army and, after demobilization, returned to lecturing in 1940 to complete the major component of his doctoral degree, published in 1945 as *Phenomenology of Perception*.

Following the success of what turned out to be his most famous publication he was appointed a Professor of Philosophy at the University of Lyon. Then from

1949 to 1952 he served as the Professor of Child Psychology and Pedagogy at the University of Paris (Sorbonne), before being awarded the prestigious Chair in Philosophy at the Collège de France, a post subsequently occupied by such intellectual luminaries as Jacques Derrida and Michel Foucault (about whom there are further volumes in the *Thinkers for Architects* series). After almost a decade of intense activity in both teaching and writing, in 1961 he died suddenly of a heart attack at the age of fifty-three, at home in his study at No. 10 Boulevard St Michel, with a copy of Descartes' *Dioptrics* left open on his desk in preparation for a lecture the following day. He left behind a number of unfinished projects, including his famously complex text 'The Intertwining – The Chiasm', which was published posthumously, along with his working notes, as part of *The Visible and the Invisible* in 1964.

In subsequent years his philosophy gradually declined in popularity, mainly owing to the rise of new intellectual trends like structuralism and poststructuralism – approaches that were (and often still are) assumed by many to be antagonistic to phenomenology. Merleau-Ponty himself would have denied this opposition, having made much use of structuralist ideas in developing his own position, including the linguistic theories of Ferdinand de Saussure, as well as the 'structural anthropology' of his good friend Claude Lévi-Strauss. In recent years Merleau-Ponty's work has undergone something of a revival, having found new audiences in a number of areas concerned with the broader implications of embodiment. These include the perhaps unlikely disciplines of cognitive science, human–computer interaction, artificial intelligence and advanced robotics, alongside the more straightforward application of his ideas to contemporary studies of consciousness, the philosophy of mind, psychology and sociology.

CHAPTER 2

# Embodied space

## It's not what you think

As I have already suggested, the 'lived body' is central to Merleau-Ponty's philosophy. This is not the body as a static object with a particular physical form or anatomical structure, but rather the body as a set of possibilities for action that we each experience for ourselves from the inside out. One might even say that for Merleau-Ponty – to use an architectural analogy that he himself may well have resisted – the body was the cornerstone of his whole philosophical project. In one sense he described it as the implicit foundation for everything we come to know about the world, and for the reader he revealed a progressively clearer picture of this typically hidden founding function. As I hope to demonstrate in different ways, in this and the chapters to follow, Merleau-Ponty helps us to understand how the body provides our only means of 'having a world', and of achieving what he called that ongoing 'gearing of the subject into his world that is the origin of space' (Merleau-Ponty 2012: 262). In this formulation we can see already why embodied experience was so fundamental to Merleau-Ponty's philosophy and why it should also be of interest to anyone concerned with the understanding and organization of space.

**This is not the body as a static object with a particular physical form or anatomical structure, but rather the body as a set of possibilities for action.**

To begin with, as a phenomenologist, Merleau-Ponty is concerned quite literally with the study of phenomena; and phenomena, in this context, are 'things as they appear to us'. The word 'phenomenology' itself originates with the Greek terms *phaino* and *logos*, where *phaino* refers to a gradual emergence or 'showing forth', as with the related English words *epiphany*, *phantom* and *fantasy*, which are all based on the same root. As a philosophical approach phenomenology concentrates on the structures and contents of consciousness; in other words, on how things in the world appear 'for us' rather than how they might actually be 'in themselves'. This may sound at first like a trivial and pedantic distinction but it is actually part of a long-standing argument about the scope and limits of philosophy, as well as about the truth-claims of science as the apparently privileged realm of ultimate knowledge.

The crux of the issue is that science purports to give us the truth about the world: precise accounts of the nature of things as they are, independent of human interference. Since the emergence of what we now call modern science in the early part of the seventeenth century, scientific investigation has been based on a rigorous method of empirical first-hand observation. Thanks largely to the work of philosophers like René Descartes in France and Francis Bacon in England, this approach to the search for knowledge quickly took over from traditional sources, such as the 'received wisdom' of ancient texts, religious belief and superstition. Despite its many obvious advances, science has been notoriously reluctant to acknowledge the unavoidable influence of the experimental observer on the outcome of the observation. It is only since the early part of the twentieth century that this issue has been openly addressed. Alongside the many examples of so-called 'observer effects' noted throughout physics, thermodynamics and quantum mechanics, there is also the related case of Werner Heisenberg's famous 'uncertainty principle', which shows that precise measurements of some related quantities are, in reality, mutually exclusive. There is also a more basic uncertainty about the fundamental nature of things exemplified in the still mysterious properties of light, which exhibits both wave and particle-like behaviour. This mystery has only deepened in recent years with ever more sophisticated observations at the sub-atomic level (Barad 2007) where certainty seems even further away than it was when Merleau-Ponty was writing.

One of the key issues that Edmund Husserl set out to address in his early work *Logical Investigations* (2001/1900), and to which he returned in his unfinished final work *The Crisis of the European Sciences* (1970/1936), is that scientific knowledge appears to rest on a number of basic premises, such as those mentioned above, that are either not declared or not properly clarified within the study of science (Husserl 2001; 1970). Aware that there was no straightforward way of resolving these questions about the ultimate nature of reality, phenomenologists have tried instead to focus their efforts towards understanding human experience, accepting that the world in itself will always exceed or *transcend* our own individual attempts to perceive it.

The other long-standing problem that phenomenology set out to tackle was the conceptual split between the mental and the physical realms, inherited from the seventeenth-century writings of Descartes. The legacy of this so-called mind–body dualism was the problem of explaining the link between these two realms, which had given rise to two opposing ways of understanding how we come to have knowledge of the world. In *Phenomenology of Perception* Merleau-Ponty claimed to have found an alternative middle way, somewhere between the two competing historical positions that he labelled Intellectualism and Realism. Realism refers to the Empirical Tradition begun by the seventeenth-century English philosopher John Locke, who described all knowledge as 'caused by' incoming sense-data bombarding the passive body. By contrast, the Intellectualist position involves the projection of pre-existing mental categories onto a basically passive world, where experience is effectively constituted by individual acts of consciousness. The distinctive aspect of Merleau-Ponty's approach – one that he shared with Martin Heidegger – was to recognize that knowledge, in fact, begins in the realm of embodied experience and only later does it become available to intellectual classification. Contrary to the common-sense perspective, where the world appears neatly divided into thinking subjects and material objects (broadly speaking, people and things), Merleau-Ponty showed that this view is actually an artificial abstraction. Beneath this intellectual overlay lies a more primordial condition, one that he described more poetically as the in-between realm of the 'flesh of the world' (Merleau-Ponty 1968: 130–162) – the realm in which bodily 'practical' experience begins and about which 'reflective' knowledge later claims to speak.

> ... it is only because we know what it feels like to occupy space by virtue of our own embodiment that we can understand the world itself as made up of material objects in space.

While it might appear that there is a contradiction in Merleau-Ponty's ambitious project – philosophizing about a realm of experience that he has already implied is beyond philosophy – his attempt to 'reflect on the unreflected' does provide a number of important insights, not least of which is a profound analysis of the intimate relation between the spatiality of the body-in-action and the spatiality of the world itself. In other words, the idea that it is only because we know what it feels like to occupy space by virtue of our own embodiment – the fact we are incarnate material beings that 'take up' space in the world – that we can understand the world itself as made up of material objects in space. This principle of 'reversibility' that Merleau-Ponty invoked to explain this two-way relation is one that we will return to in Chapter 4, in relation to the discussion of materiality in architecture. For now it is enough to note that he also applied this theory to perception in general, in his claim that we perceive the world only by virtue of our body's own perceptibility.

He illustrated this idea with the example of the body in contact with itself, such as when the right hand touches the left hand and there are two simultaneous sensations. In this situation Merleau-Ponty claimed there is an important exchange of information; a kind of feedback loop that allows one perception to be 'confirmed' by the data from the other (Merleau-Ponty 2012: 94f). The philosopher David Morris has called this the 'crossing of body and world', in the sense that our interaction with any object will always yield a curiously hybrid perception: while we may think that when we have touched an object we have experienced the object *in itself*, this is in fact slightly misleading, as what we have really perceived is the *interaction* between the object and our own active body (Morris 2004: 4f). It is therefore only by virtue of the body's own materiality that we are able to have this encounter with material things: a disembodied mind, if there could even be such a thing, would have no means of access to the world. In other words, rather than saying that one thing (the body) perceives another thing (the object) – or even vice versa – it would be more correct to say that they are both partaking equally in the phenomenon of perceptibility:

> ... the thickness of flesh between the seer and the thing is constitutive for the thing of its visibility as for the seer of his corporeity; it is not an obstacle between them, it is their means of communication. ... The thickness of the body, far from rivalling that of the world, is on the contrary the sole means I have to go unto the heart of things ...
>
> (Merleau-Ponty 1968: 135)

For those Idealist philosophers who feared being misled by the bodily senses, the solution was to retreat to the apparently comforting certainty of the inner world of mental processes. Hence Descartes' famous statement, 'I think therefore I am', or, more precisely: 'I am thinking, therefore I exist' (Descartes 1985: 127). For Merleau-Ponty, on the other hand, far from being a source of inaccuracy and error, the sensory information provided by the body is actually our primary source of knowledge: not a *barrier* but a *bridge* to the world.

## Body schemas

To understand how we gain access to the world through the activity of the moving body it is important to first appreciate that the lived body provides a distinctive form of conscious awareness. More typical for phenomenological thinkers is the understanding of consciousness in terms of 'intentionality'; the idea that when we are conscious we are always *conscious of* something, so it is never an empty or contentless state. This 'thing' that consciousness is directed towards may be either an object 'out there' in the world or a subjective inner awareness of an emotional or mental state. The novelty of Merleau-Ponty's approach was to propose a more primary form of awareness: a 'bodily intentionality' that provides our initial grasp or sense of a situation, allowing us to cope with the ongoing flow of experience. This kind of implicit or intuitive awareness that precedes intellectual analysis is also what allows us to perform one activity 'in the background' while attending explicitly to another. For example, imagine all the bodily movements involved in driving a car safely, which experienced motorists can do quite easily while carrying on a deep conversation with a passenger. This bodily ability to function in a spatial situation operates below the level of what we would normally call conscious awareness, but it gives us a way of explaining our underlying orientation in the world that allows us to grasp or 'cope with' experience as it gradually unfolds around us.

## The novelty of Merleau-Ponty's approach was to propose a more primary form of awareness: a 'bodily intentionality' that provides our initial grasp or sense of a situation, allowing us to cope with the ongoing flow of experience.

A key component of this form of bodily awareness is the sense of our own physical limits and capacities. To explain this Merleau-Ponty borrowed a notion from previous research in psychology regarding the function of the so-called 'body schema', first described by the English neurologists Henry Head and Gordon Holmes in 1911, and cited in *Phenomenology of Perception* (Merleau-Ponty 2012: 31, 123, 142). Despite the confusion caused by one of Merleau-Ponty's earlier translators in rendering the French term *schéma corporel* as the rather misleading 'body image', the key thing for Merleau-Ponty is that the schema is neither a static template nor a visual image lodged in the brain. Instead, body schemas emerge and evolve gradually over time, as a consequence of our ongoing engagement with the world. This process relies on what is called 'proprioception': our inbuilt sense of the body's orientation and position in space, as well as the relation of one body part to another. Proprioceptive awareness results from the coordination of data from a number of bodily systems, including the kinaesthetic (musculo-skeletal) and vestibular (inner ear), which together provide us with a sense of motion, direction and balance. This information is processed in the brain to help us monitor our ongoing movement, giving us the means to adjust our behaviour in order to achieve our intended goals. Repeated movements gradually coalesce into 'sedimented' skills or patterns of behaviour, which in turn provide an implicit awareness of our own body's possibilities for action in a given environment. A useful explanation of this process has recently been given by the American philosopher Shaun Gallagher, showing how Merleau-Ponty's dynamic understanding of the body schema even anticipates some recent developments in neuroscience (Gallagher 2005).

Merleau-Ponty often supported his explanations with evidence drawn from clinical cases, including, for example, the study of the German soldier Johann Schneider, who had suffered a brain injury during the First World War. While Schneider was unable to move parts of his body when explicitly instructed to do so, he could control them perfectly well when acting out complex movements he had learned before his injury. Damage to his visual cortex had disrupted the vital link between his visual and tactile systems, preventing the normal interaction that allows the body schema to be consciously adapted to new situations (Merleau-Ponty 2012: 105f). Likewise, Merleau-Ponty also made reference to the phenomenon of 'phantom limb', where an amputee experiences pain in a limb that has been surgically removed. In these cases the patient's conscious visual perception comes into conflict with the body schema, with the result that the explicit visual evidence of the missing limb is overridden by the unconscious body schema that often remains stubbornly intact (Merleau-Ponty 2012: 101f). Contemporary neuroscience has again confirmed much of Merleau-Ponty's interpretation, as for example in the famous work of Vilayanur Ramachandran, who uses mirrors to help patients recover control over a troublesome phantom limb (Ramachandran 2003: 1–27).

So, for Merleau-Ponty the body schema is actually a complex network of interrelated patterns: effectively a whole array of 'body schemas' to suit the demands of specific situations. This idea is important for Merleau-Ponty because it forms the basis for a new definition of the self, based on the principle that to be embodied is to be always already engaged with the world. For Merleau-Ponty therefore, embodiment already implies 'emplacement' (Pink 2011), that sense of embeddedness in a social and spatial context out of which our individual subjectivity is gradually constituted. In contrast to Descartes' 'thinking subject' as a detached and rational entity, Merleau-Ponty proposes a self that is defined not by what it *is*, as such, but instead by what it can *do*, referring directly to the terms used by Husserl in his discussion of the body's capacity for movement: '… these clarifications allow us to understand motricity [the faculty or power of movement] unequivocally as original intentionality. Consciousness is originally not an "I think that", but rather an "I can"' (Merleau-Ponty 2012: 139).

In contrast to Descartes' 'thinking subject' as a detached and rational entity, Merleau-Ponty proposes a self that is defined not by what it *is*, as such, but instead by what it can *do*.

### Motor cognition

The idea of body schemas also helps explain how we can apparently experience a so-called 'percept' without first invoking a concept, in the sense that our bodily recognition of the 'look and feel' of a situation is what first allows us to begin to make sense of it. This kind of global recognition of a certain type or 'category' of space sets up a bodily anticipation of what we are about to experience. Consequently, we should think of a body schema not as a 'model' of the world as such, but rather as a means of dealing with it. As a set of acquired skills and patterns of behaviour it allows us to navigate in a range of environments, where each one is encountered as the background to the performance of a particular task. It is this task – or function of the space – that is the usual focus of our conscious attention, and those parts of the body not directly involved could be said to 'withdraw' from our immediate awareness. Likewise, the background elements of the space will also effectively 'disappear' from view:

> Psychologists often say that the body schema is *dynamic*. Reduced to a precise sense, this term means that my body appears to me as a posture toward a certain task, actual or possible. And in fact my body's spatiality is not, like the spatiality of external objects or of 'spatial sensations', a *positional spatiality*; rather, it is a *situational spatiality*. If I stand in front of my desk and lean on it with both hands, only my hands are accentuated and my whole body trails behind them like a comet's tail. I am not unaware of the location of my shoulders or my waist; rather, this awareness is enveloped in my awareness of my hands and my entire stance is read, so to speak, in how my hands lean upon the desk.
>
> (Merleau-Ponty 2012: 102)

It is this task-oriented aspect of perception that should be of particular interest to architects and designers, and I will return to this theme later in relation to the formal expression of building functions. For now the key thing to take on board is the way in which body schemas operate in a temporal capacity, as part of an ongoing process of pattern recognition based on the accumulation of previous experiences. Thus, rather than the conscious application of concepts which would take too long to 'bring online', the urgency of our unfolding experience demands a much more immediate means of 'sense-making'. Therefore our initial understanding of the meaning of a situation (i.e. our sense of what is going on right now, and how to deal with it) actually comes about through what Merleau-Ponty called 'motor cognition': a pre-reflective bodily grip on the world as a set of structured arenas for action. The body therefore serves as a kind of 'cognitive flywheel' maintaining the momentum of our ongoing actions, allowing time for our conscious awareness to gradually process experience in more abstract conceptual terms. This motor-cognitive form of awareness draws on our continually evolving history of previous experiences, giving us a bodily ability to respond to the 'solicitations of the world' to act in a particular way. This is an idea that Merleau-Ponty also partly inherited from the French philosopher Henri Bergson who, in his early book *Matter and Memory* (1896), suggested that: 'The objects which surround my body reflect its possible action upon them' (Bergson 1988/1896: 21). This idea was also later echoed by the American psychologist James J. Gibson in his concept of environmental 'affordances'; those opportunities for action that spaces offer us and which are partly dependent on our bodily abilities to engage with them (Gibson 1986: 127–143). For Merleau-Ponty this means that the body schema, as we have described above, is partly structured from within and partly from the 'outside-in':

> What counts for the orientation of the spectacle is not my body, such as it in fact exists, as a thing in objective space, but rather my body as a system of possible actions, a virtual body whose phenomenal 'place' is defined by its task and by its situation.
>
> (Merleau-Ponty 2012: 260)

The body therefore serves as a kind of 'cognitive flywheel' maintaining the momentum of our ongoing actions, allowing time for our conscious awareness to gradually process experience in more abstract conceptual terms.

Just as the principle of intentionality means that consciousness is always a 'consciousness of' something, for Merleau-Ponty our grasp of a space is always as a 'situation for' some activity or another. In his first book, *The Structure of Behavior,* he gave the following example of someone 'reading' a space as a field of opportunities for action:

> For the player in action the football field is not an 'object', ... It is pervaded with lines of force (the 'yard lines'; those which demarcate the 'penalty area') and articulated in sectors (for example, the 'openings' between the adversaries) which will call for a certain mode of action and which initiate and guide the action as if the player were unaware of it. The field itself is not given to him, ... the player becomes one with it and feels the direction of the

'goal', for example, just as immediately as the vertical and the horizontal planes of his own body.

(Merleau-Ponty 1963: 168)

While this may seem like an extreme case of a 'structured arena for action' it is still a useful example of how body schemas depend on acquired habits or behavioural patterns. As Merleau-Ponty suggests, it is only through habit that we acquire the ability to 'in-habit' space, as familiarity allows us to navigate easily and to focus instead on the task in hand. In spaces that we use frequently, we have an implicit bodily awareness of where objects are located, so we can move around relatively easily without conscious effort:

When I move about in my house, I know immediately and without any intervening discourse that to walk toward the bathroom involves passing close to the bedroom, or that to look out the window involves having the fireplace to my left. In this small world, each gesture or each perception is immediately situated in relation to a thousand virtual coordinates.

(Merleau-Ponty 2012: 131)

Both of the above examples hint at the curiously hybrid status of so-called 'practical knowledge', which for Merleau-Ponty involved a combination of two ways of knowing, which are often seen in opposition. I am referring here to the distinction made famous by the British philosopher Gilbert Ryle in his book *The Concept of Mind,* first published in 1949. Ryle suggested a fundamental difference between what he called 'knowing how' (i.e. having the practical ability to perform a particular action), and 'knowing that' such-and-such a thing is true or false (Ryle 1963: 28–32). The definitions are useful in reminding us of what is distinctive about bodily knowledge in the sense that a skill is something that cannot be simply described or translated into factual statements. For example, reading a book about the process of learning to play the piano is not the same thing as actually learning to do it. Merleau-Ponty's analysis of motor cognition also suggested further that the ability to function in the world involves both *knowing how* to do something and *knowing when* to do it. Take, for example, a rock climber's ability to climb a particular rock face. This involves both the ability to climb rock faces in general – at least up to a certain level of difficulty – as well as the climber's ability to identify this particular one as being within their capability. We might also add that motor cognition therefore involves both physical and social awareness: recognizing *that* the environment affords an opportunity to act in a particular way, as well as knowing *when* it might actually be appropriate to do so.

### Place and memory

The previous point should also remind us that even factual or propositional knowledge still has an important bodily aspect, in the sense that knowing a fact involves more than simply being able to recall it from memory. Crucially, it also means knowing how – and when – to employ it; in other words, knowing its relevance to a particular social or cultural context. This idea has been influential in recent education theory under the banner of 'situated learning', where teaching either takes place in classrooms set up to mimic real-world conditions, or out 'on the job' itself, where the knowledge learned will ultimately be applied (Lave and Wenger 1991). It is now clear that the context in which learning takes place has a powerful effect on the ability to retain and recall it, highlighting an important fact about the relation between place and memory that has a number of architectural consequences. This is an idea that was first formalized in ancient Roman times among teachers of the art of oratory, who developed a technique for memorizing long speeches based on re-enacting imaginary journeys. By associating passages or episodes from a text with a sequence of spaces from a well-known building, they could deliver a speech from memory simply by imagining themselves retracing the route (Yates 1992: 17–20).

> Propositional knowledge still has an important bodily aspect, in the sense that knowing a fact involves more than simply being able to recall it from memory. Crucially, it also means knowing how – and when – to employ it.

If remembering involves a form of re-enactment of the experience in which knowledge was originally acquired – as recent developments in the neuroscience of memory have also begun to suggest (Rose 2003: 375–381) – then there are at least two important bodily dimensions to this ability to recall facts. One is the sense in which all knowledge is in some way *situational*, and is therefore both linked to and triggered by the context in which it was learned. As Merleau-Ponty suggested: 'This is clearly what Bergson means when he speaks of a "motor structure" of recollection' (Merleau-Ponty 2012: 186), implying that the act of remembering actually involves a process of 're-experiencing'. The other is that knowledge also carries a characteristic *emotional* charge: what the neuroscientist Antonio Damasio has recently described as a distinctive 'somatic marker' (Damasio 2000: 40–42). One illustration of this is the fact that traumatic experiences are particularly difficult to forget, often resulting in the most vivid recollections of seemingly insignificant details.

On the positive side, habit gives us the bodily skills we need to function efficiently in our everyday environment. As we saw above, Merleau-Ponty was able to move about in his apartment in the dark without having to think too carefully about how he was actually doing it. At the same time this familiarity can also 'breed contempt', in the sense that we gradually come to ignore many of the details of our everyday surroundings. At the level of sensory perception this effect also appears in what psychologists call 'habituation'; the ability of the body to gradually damp down responses to a continually repeated stimulus. While this can allow us to shut out distractions like annoying background noise in a busy restaurant, the downside is that we need to keep increasing a stimulus if we want to remain aware of it. A more obvious case of habituation occurs when we touch the surface of a textured object: unless we keep moving our fingers the sensation of roughness quickly fades away. Merleau-Ponty also extended this explanation to a more active form of vision which he likewise claimed depends on maintaining bodily movement: '… every focusing act must be renewed, otherwise it falls into the unconscious. The object only remains clear in front of me if I scan it with my eyes …' (Merleau-Ponty 2012: 249). In other words, when we fix our gaze upon a random point in space the visual scene gradually flattens out and loses much of its depth and colour, especially towards the outer edges, as has been shown by more recent experiments (Livingstone 2002: 74–76).

## From Bauhaus to Koolhaas

It is easy to see how the successful use of a building relies on recognizing clues to the function of a space. And it would therefore be all too easy to take this idea as support for the doctrine of functional expression in architecture. Modernist architecture is often described as the attempt to make form 'follow function', so that users could anticipate what kind of activities are likely to be going on inside a building. One issue that arises when this correlation gets too close is that spaces become very difficult to adapt to other functions. This can be a major problem for multi-use spaces that may need to be transformed on a daily basis. A parallel tendency in recent history – from Mies van der Rohe to Rem Koolhaas – is to move towards a kind of loose-fitting or 'universal space' that avoids any obvious functional symbolism. The downside of this approach is that buildings can end up as characterless boxes, where the anonymity of the environment provides little stimulation to the creative activity of its users. To counter this tendency writers such as Stewart Brand and Fred Scott have suggested that buildings should be designed to accommodate a range of different cycles of change, encapsulated in Brand's notion of 'shearing layers', from the scale of mobile furniture up to permanent structural elements (Brand 1994: 13). In this case, functional affordances can also be more directly expressed at the level of interior design, allowing for adaptations to occur more easily to accommodate changes in the use of the space.

Other approaches which avoid some of these problems include what might be called the 'critical functionalism' of American architect Peter Eisenman, who often aims both to express and to challenge expectations by deliberately disrupting conventional uses. His most obvious – and not particularly subtle – example was in the now famous House VI, where the geometric composition of overlaid grids resulted in a slot being cut through the middle of a double bed. The point for Eisenman was not to deny but rather to inspire the user's creative occupation of the space, providing a stimulus – some would even say an irritant

– to provoke some previously untried pattern of behaviour. A similar thing seems to happen with the adaptive reuse of historic buildings, where traces of previous uses are often still visible alongside the more obvious signs of the new function. These cases also offer invitations to the active engagement of the creative user, and I will return to discuss this in more detail in terms of creativity in general in Chapter 4.

> The point for Eisenman was not to deny but rather to inspire the user's creative occupation of the space.

## The social body

Defining the self as an 'I can' as opposed to an 'I am' puts the embodied self at centre stage as an active agent in the world. Indeed, Merleau-Ponty adopted Heidegger's use of the term 'being in the world' to describe one of the main themes of his philosophical project. The language is important here because it encapsulates a central principle in both philosophers' work: the idea that we cannot study the nature of human 'being' in isolation from the rest of the world. Hence, the name 'Existential Phenomenology', which is often used to distinguish their work from that of Husserl, although it is Sartre's related philosophy of individual freedom that probably best deserves this label. What made Merleau-Ponty's work distinctive was his concern with that primordial state of continuity that exists between the body and its environment, prior to the artificial conceptual division of subject and object. In this project, he set himself in opposition to the whole tradition of 'objective thought':

> The consistent function of objective thought is to reduce all of the phenomena that attest to the union of the subject and the world, and to substitute for them the clear idea of the object as an *in-itself* and of the subject as a pure consciousness.
>
> (Merleau-Ponty 2012: 334)

For Merleau-Ponty, much more than Heidegger, we have seen already how everything began with the lived body. However, it would be a mistake to interpret this as a claim for the dominance of individual subjectivity. While it is fair to say that Merleau-Ponty often appeared to underplay the central role of social structures in the formation of the self, considering his work as a whole it is clear that this remained a key part of his analysis. It is important to remember that body schemas are not simply projections outward of physical or behavioural capacities; rather they are determined as much from the *outside in* as they are from the inside out. This logic is based on the fact that we each develop body schemas as we learn to interact with the world around us; a world that is already collectively structured by the people who have existed before us. Perception in general, for Merleau-Ponty, was likewise an acquired collection of skills, a certain 'style' of bodily comportment – a mode or manner of being – that responds to what he called the solicitations of the world around us. The concept of the body schema is therefore closely related to what has also been called the *habitus*; a term used by both Husserl and Merleau-Ponty but made famous later by the sociologist Pierre Bourdieu. For Bourdieu the habitus is the set of habits, dispositions and practices prevalent among particular groups, although it is never clearly explained how the transition between collective and individual takes place. While he described it as both a structured and a 'structuring structure' (Bourdieu 1990: 53), he tended to overemphasize its controlling effect on behaviour, downplaying the role of individuals in the continual restructuring of these collective structures. For Merleau-Ponty it is precisely the body that enables us to 'fight back' against the imposition of social rules and, in his late essay, 'On the Phenomenology of Language', he provided a more convincing model of how social systems dynamically evolve (Merleau-Ponty 1964c: 84–97). I will return to this argument later in discussing how designers can also challenge architectural conventions, but for now it is important to appreciate how the body schema allows us to 'meet the world halfway':

> **For if it is true that I am conscious of my body through the world and if my body is the unperceived term at the center of the world toward which every**

object turns its face, then it is true for the same reason that my body is the pivot of the world.

(Merleau-Ponty 2012: 84)

Body schemas are not simply projections outward of physical or behavioural capacities, rather they are determined as much from the *outside in* as they are from the inside out.

As we saw previously in the example of the football pitch, the players must continually respond to the opportunities presented, with each of them effectively 'creating' themselves as successful footballers on the basis of the collective success of the team as a whole. Likewise in society in general we find ourselves thrown into a 'game' already under way, where all the players are following rules that have been established by others before us. We have no choice in this situation but to try to work out for ourselves what might be going on, by observing what the other players are doing and then trying our best to join in. The creative aspect of this process is that – unlike in football – each player is also gradually rewriting the rules, because the rules only exist in their continual reproduction through the players' actions, through the rather imprecise and inaccurate form of individual bodily performance. Thus, the habitus, even in Bourdieu's terminology, is a fundamentally unstable structure because each of our attempts to reproduce it is never quite as accurate as we might intend. As Merleau-Ponty suggested: 'History, then, is neither a perpetual novelty nor a perpetual repetition, but rather the unique movement that both creates stable forms and shatters them.' (Merleau-Ponty 2012: 90). He was perhaps clearest on this point when he was discussing the gradual evolution of language, when he described a similar process of modification which happens when anyone makes use of the system. This process of gradual mutation takes place through what he called 'coherent deformation'; those often minute changes in meaning that come about through the way in which each individual act of speaking is realized.

Thus we might even say that as functional spaces offer affordances for action, so language in a similar way offers affordances for communication. The unique ways in which each of us takes up and exploits these opportunities – as when we inflect our language with a particular intonation or gestural emphasis – can also have a profound impact on how others interpret our actions. It is these gradual slippages of meaning that also add new components to the system, enlarging the canon of available meanings, as Peter Eisenman was aiming to do. I will return to this discussion of language in Chapter 5 on creativity and innovation in design, but for now the key thing to notice is Merleau-Ponty's sensibility regarding socially structured systems: 'To learn to speak is to learn to play a series of *roles*, to assume a series of conducts or linguistic gestures.' (Merleau-Ponty 1964a: 109). In taking this view he was influenced strongly by his reading of the Swiss linguistic philosopher Ferdinand de Saussure (widely acknowledged as the source of what became known as 'structural linguistics'), not to mention the impact of his long-standing friendship with the structural anthropologist Claude Lévi-Strauss, who dedicated his major work, *The Savage Mind* from 1962, 'to the Memory of Maurice Merleau-Ponty'. While many later commentators preferred to overlook this important social dimension of Merleau-Ponty's thought, some important recovery work has been done by recent British sociologists reassessing his influence on later thinkers like Bourdieu (Burkitt 1999; Crossley 2001).

There is also another aspect to this apparent mismatch between intention and realization, seen for example in the familiar inability of language to capture our deeper emotions or fleeting impressions. A similar gap appears in the always slightly unsatisfactory performance of a building that was originally designed to accommodate only an idealized version of its intended function. A more positive consequence of those moments when the world seems to 'get in the way' of our best intentions is that we are reminded that we are, after all, living embodied beings in a world of other beings and material objects. This is what the American Pragmatist philosopher John Dewey described as the somewhat paradoxical value of a world that pushes back against our attempts to transform it, reminding us that we are alive and at the same time teaching us something vital about our own capacities and limits:

> The only way [the living organism] can become aware of its nature and its goal is by obstacles surmounted and means employed; means which are only means from the very beginning are too much one with an impulsion, on a way smoothed and oiled in advance, to permit of consciousness of them. Nor without resistance from surroundings would the self become aware of itself.
>
> (Dewey 1980/1934: 59)

A simple architectural example of this occurs in the everyday act of opening a door. In addition to the texture and quality of the handle, we also feel the weight and balance of the door, which gives us an implicit sense of what we might expect to find inside, based on our existing stock of bodily memories. As Juhani Pallasmaa has usefully noted, the door handle is 'the handshake of a building' (Pallasmaa 2005: 61), offering a first intimation of the character of a space that can be either confirmed or denied by our subsequent experience.

## Both built spaces and languages could be described as socially structured systems that we have to actively 'take up' – and therefore coherently deform – each time we try to use them.

### From the extended body to the extended mind

As we have just seen, both built spaces and languages could be described as socially structured systems that we have to actively 'take up' – and therefore coherently deform – each time we try to use them for our own purposes. The 'world' that results from these encounters is, of course, equally dependent on the particular configuration of our own embodiment. To explain this Merleau-Ponty – as we have seen already – borrowed the concept of the *Umwelt* ('surrounding world') from Jakob von Uexküll, discussing the idea at length in one of his lectures on *Nature* given at the Collège de France in the late 1950s (Merleau-Ponty 2003: 167–178). The concept involves a new understanding of how all living organisms effectively 'specify' their own environment:

> The *Umwelt* marks the difference between the world such as it exists in itself, and the world as the world of a living being. It is an intermediary reality between the world as it exists for an absolute observer and a purely subjective domain. It is the aspect of the world in itself to which the animal addresses itself, which exists for the behavior of an animal.
>
> (Merleau-Ponty 2003: 167)

Uexküll surmised that each particular species effectively exists in its own specific environment, defined partly by what it can *do*, and equally by what it can *perceive*. Both of these factors are constrained by the organism's specific physiological capacities; the layout of its basic 'body plan' and the configuration of its sensory systems. Pigeons, for example, are pentachromats, meaning that they see the world in five 'primary colours', while cats and bats can detect high-frequency sounds well above the threshold of human hearing. Dogs – and of course many other species – exist in worlds structured primarily by olfactory signals, while some rainforest monkeys live solely within the tree canopy and never set foot on the ground. Each of these animals effectively inhabits a kind of parallel universe, albeit that they are still able to encounter each other in their overlapping physical spaces. Uexküll also produced some useful descriptions of how the world might appear to a different form of perception, along with a fascinating series of diagrams first published in 1934 (Uexküll 2010: 61–70). As Merleau-Ponty wrote in *The Structure of Behavior*: '… the organism itself measures the action of things upon it and itself delimits its milieu by a circular process' (Merleau-Ponty 1983: 148). In other words, we could say that different forms of embodiment effectively open up different forms of environment. As we saw earlier with the unfortunate case of Schneider – as well as with amputees suffering from 'phantom limb' – bodily deficits can radically alter the ability to engage with and occupy space.

One of Merleau-Ponty's best known and perhaps most influential ideas emerged from his analysis of the experience of tools, where he described the process by which they become 'incorporated' into body schemas. While his discussion echoed that of Heidegger in his famous analysis from *Being and Time* (Heidegger 1962: 95–107) Merleau-Ponty developed the argument much further in relation to the nuances of bodily experience. His now classic example of the way a tool is incorporated into an extended body schema considered a blind person learning to navigate with the aid of a white cane (Merleau-Ponty 2012: 153). By moving the cane across the ground surface, information is gradually gathered in, effectively extending the sensitivity of the blind person's hand out towards the tip of the cane. By experiencing the tactile sensations – alongside the acoustic feedback – a three-dimensional environment begins to be revealed, while the cane effectively 'disappears' from the user's perception. As Merleau-Ponty suggested, with skilful use the tool itself ceases to be a direct object of experience and becomes instead a 'medium' through which we can experience the world – just as, by analogy, we experience through the body itself:

> **Habit does not *consist* in interpreting the pressure of the cane on the hand like signs of certain positions of the cane, and then these positions as signs of an external object – for the habit *relieves us* of this very task. ... the cane is no longer an object that the blind man would perceive, it has become an instrument *with* which he perceives.**
>
> (Merleau-Ponty 2012: 152f)

The use of all kinds of tools and equipment is therefore gradually sedimented into habits or behavioural routines, withdrawing from direct awareness to become part of our bodily repertoire of skills and abilities. We might also argue that this is similar to how most people – especially non-architects – encounter a building: not as an object of focused attention, nor as an 'invisible' or anonymous background. Rather we mainly experience the built environment through a form of bodily cognition, as a medium *through* which we experience the task we happen to be engaged in – and, of course, as a key part of what gives that experience its characteristic quality or texture.

## We experience the built environment through a form of bodily cognition, as a medium through which we experience the task we happen to be engaged in.

The other aspect of Merleau-Ponty's analysis is that it questioned the conventional definition of the boundary between the body and the world. Common sense, of course, suggests that we know precisely where this dividing line is, but again it was John Dewey who had already challenged this naïve assumption, proposing instead a new understanding of the 'extended self' to include both our physical and our social attachments:

> The epidermis is only in the most superficial way an indication of where an organism ends and its environment begins. There are things inside the body that are foreign to it, and there are things outside of it that belong to it *de jure* if not *de facto*; that must, that is, be taken possession of if life is to continue. On the lower scale, air and food materials are such things; on the higher, tools, whether the pen of the writer or the anvil of the blacksmith, utensils and furnishings, property, friends and institutions – all the supports and sustenances without which a civilised life cannot be.
>
> **(Dewey 1980/1934: 59)**

A more recent illustration of this permeability of the boundaries between brain, body and world can be seen in the experiment carried out by the Australian performance artist Stelarc, adding a prosthetic 'Third Hand' to his own biological body (Massumi 1998: 336). The hand was controlled by nerve impulses picked up from surface electrodes attached to his thigh, and while it took some time to learn how to operate – by a process of trial-and-error experiment – eventually it could be precisely controlled, independently of the artist's other hands. This example also reminds us of the fact that from birth onwards we have all been through a similar process of bodily training, swinging our limbs about in a more or less random fashion until we gradually learned how to control and apply them. And ultimately, of course, how to reach out and take up other bits of the world in order to further extend our bodily capacities.

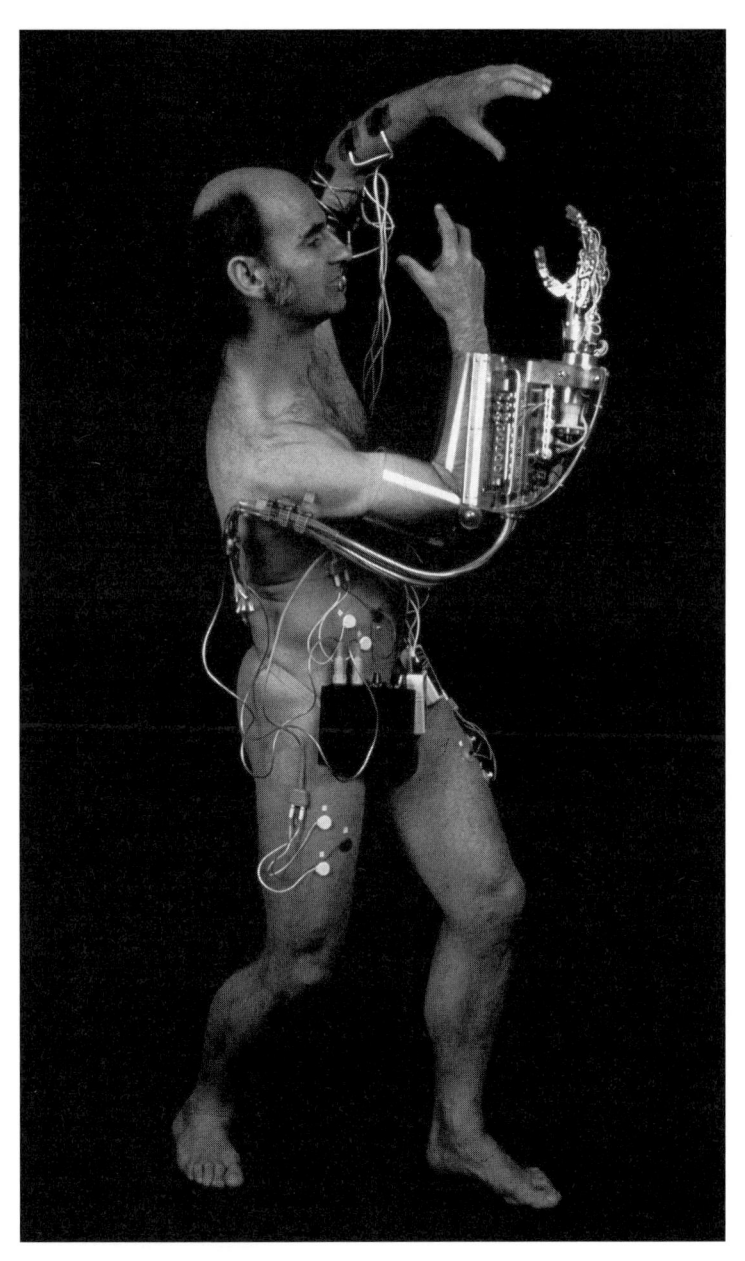

Stelarc – THIRD HAND, Tokyo, Yokohama, Nagoya 1980.

From birth onwards we have all been through a similar process of bodily training, swinging our limbs about in a more or less random fashion until we gradually learned how to control and apply them.

Incorporation of the 'tool habit' into the body schema involves what the American philosopher Hubert Dreyfus has called the process of 'skilful coping', leading to a modification in patterns of movement involved in wielding the tool effectively. Merleau-Ponty also described examples of more short-term adaptations, such as happen when we are driving a car which is larger than the one we are familiar with, or even wearing clothes that restrict or affect our movements: 'Without any explicit calculation, a woman maintains a safe distance between the feather in her hat and objects that might damage it; she senses where the feather is, just as we sense were our hand is' (Merleau-Ponty 2012: 144). In addition to these situations where the tool is subject to *incorporation*, Merleau-Ponty also described examples of what David Morris has called *excorporation* – where the body is effectively absorbed within a larger spatial environment (Morris 2004: 131), such as the cockpit of an aeroplane or the workshop of a joiner.

The key to understanding this idea is through Merleau-Ponty's notion of 'motor space', which helped him explain how tasks like typing illustrate the difference between 'knowing that' and 'knowing how':

> One can know how to type without knowing how to indicate where on the keyboard the letters that compose the words are located ... The subject knows where the letters are on the keyboard just as we know where one of our limbs is ... The subject who learns to type literally incorporates the space of the keyboard into his bodily space.
>
> (Merleau-Ponty 2012: 145f)

In this situation the skilled typist simply sees thoughts appearing on the screen as the keyboard withdraws from direct perception in favour of the task of writing. Musicians also experience this effect of what is sometimes described as a seamless 'flow', which demonstrated even more clearly for Merleau-Ponty 'how habit resides neither in thought nor in the objective body, but rather in the body as a mediator of a world' (Merleau-Ponty 2012:146). He then goes on to describe how a church organist might prepare to perform on an unfamiliar organ: 'He sits on the bench, engages the pedals, and pulls out the stops, he sizes up the instrument with his body, he incorporates its directions and dimensions, and he settles into the organ as one settles into a house' (Merleau-Ponty 2012: 146).

The pivotal role of habit as the means by which we 'in-habit' space is again seen as being based on the primary spatiality of our own embodiment, which is also extendable out into the world by means of the tools that we skilfully 'take up':

> **To habituate oneself to a hat, an automobile, or a cane is to take up residence in them, or inversely, to make them participate in the voluminosity of one's own body. Habit expresses the power we have of dilating our being in the world, or of altering our existence through incorporating new instruments.**
>
> **(Merleau-Ponty 2012: 145)**

By using the term 'altering our existence' Merleau-Ponty has drawn attention to an aspect of embodiment that has far-reaching implications. For architects this should remind us – as with Uexküll's concept of *Umwelt* – that each of us, by virtue of our own embodiment, inhabits a somewhat unique environment. Despite the superficial similarity of our human biophysical make-up, we each have particular limits in terms of our everyday skills and capacities. In addition to this, many building users have more dramatic physical limitations, such as motor, perceptual or cognitive deficits caused by long-term illness or disability. Architects have traditionally been very neglectful of what are often seen as 'problem cases', but in recent years a resurgence of interest in the body has done much to heighten awareness of these issues. Merleau-Ponty's work should also remind us that there is no clear boundary between 'abled' and 'disabled' users, and that everyone in society can gain from a more nuanced understanding of the role of embodiment.

> Merleau-Ponty's work should also remind us that there is no clear boundary between 'abled' and 'disabled' users, and that everyone in society can gain from a more nuanced understanding of the role of embodiment.

Another aspect of this notion of 'alteration' is the fear that we are being somehow dehumanized by technology and this has been a major theme in twentieth-century philosophy, including in the work of Heidegger (Heidegger 1977: 3–35; Borgmann 1984; Postman 1993). More recent writers have been tempted to identify a new 'posthuman' condition, where the boundaries between the artificial and natural are becoming ever more difficult to define: witness, for example, the advances in gene therapy, cloning, artificial intelligence and prosthetics (Braidotti 2013). In my view Merleau-Ponty has shown us that this is far from a new phenomenon; that in fact this is already an intrinsic part of what it is to be a human being. As the French philosopher Bernard Stiegler has also more recently claimed: 'The prosthesis is not a mere extension of the human body; it is the constitution of this body qua "human"' (Stiegler 1998: 152). In other words, as Merleau-Ponty described, to be human is to be already extended – or 'dilated' – into the world. By reaching out to engage with the environment through both our bodily and technical extensions we are fulfilling rather than denying the nature of what it is to be a human being.

In addition to the more obvious physical benefits of tools like pens and hammers to which John Dewey referred, it is important to appreciate that these extensions can also offer cognitive advantages. The philosophers Andy Clark and

David Chalmers have recently coined the term 'extended mind' to explain how even simple technologies can act as 'cognitive scaffolding' to the thinking process (Menary 2010). They describe how we commonly rely on various technical props and supports to help us to deal with everyday mental tasks, from notepads and pencils for writing down ideas to electronic calculators and digital search engines for retrieving and manipulating useful information. The all-too-familiar misfortune of losing a wallet or a mobile phone also reminds us how distressing it is to be denied access to what can suddenly seem like a vital organ. Robbed of our taken-for-granted ability to look up addresses, check diary entries, make phone calls and access the Internet, it is easy to feel that we are not quite the complete person that we previously assumed we were. And if we accept that, at the larger scale, even buildings can help us to think, this idea could have important implications for how architects approach interior design; for example, in reconfiguring spaces to assist people suffering from age-related cognitive decline, as well as those workplace designers looking to increase the productivity of their staff (Kirsh 1995).

## Philosophers Andy Clark and David Chalmers have recently coined the term 'extended mind' to explain how even simple technologies can act as 'cognitive scaffolding' to the thinking process.

All of the above examples point to a fundamental characteristic of human behaviour: the notion that intelligence is the outcome of an ongoing engagement of the body in the world. In recent years a consensus has begun to emerge on this idea under the banner of so-called 'embodied cognitive science', which has had a major impact on how people think about human evolution, as well as how to develop artificial intelligence. In evolutionary theory the central idea is to consider the pivotal role played by early technology, particularly the selective pressure created by the possession of skills in both making and using tools. Currently, so-called cognitive archaeologists, as well as language theorists, have made a strong case for what has been called *The Cultural Origins of Human Cognition* (Tomasello 1999).

Artificial intelligence has been moving away from writing software programs that are still basically just very rapid calculators towards the creation of physical devices that are able to learn from their encounters with real-world environments (Pfeifer et al. 2007). The American philosopher Shaun Gallagher has drawn a number of these themes together in his book *How the Body Shapes the Mind* (Gallagher 2005) and, more recently, has set out the key principles of what he calls the '4E' model of cognition. With reference to the pivotal contribution of Merleau-Ponty, as well as recent advances in neuroscience, he explains how human thinking is not an isolated process 'inside the head', but rather happens in the curious nexus created by the interaction of brain, body and world. Cognition is, therefore, on the 4E principle, understood very much in Merleau-Ponty's terms, as both 'embodied' and 'extended' in the manner we have just described above, but also 'embedded' (or situated) in the context of its worldly surroundings, and also continually 'enacted' as part of an ongoing process unfolding over time (Clark 2008; Noë 2009; Rowlands 2010).

**Each time we open our eyes on the world we are thrown back into a state of 'con-fusion', and our status as independent selves has to be continually rediscovered in the unfolding of experience.**

To round off this chapter it is worth recalling one of Merleau-Ponty's founding principles; the idea that intelligence is an emergent property of embodied engagement in the material world. It is this idea of gradual emergence through an ongoing process of exploration and discovery that we can see reiterated across different timescales in terms of both evolutionary and individual development. Part of what we acquire from this process of emergence is an intellectual grasp of ourselves as distinct entities, although, as Merleau-Ponty has been careful to point out, this is never a once-and-for-all achievement. Each time we open our eyes on the world we are, in a sense, thrown back into a state of 'con-fusion', and our status as independent selves has to be continually rediscovered in the unfolding of experience:

> **Experience reveals, beneath the objective space in which the body eventually finds its place, a primordial spatiality of which objective space is but the envelope and which merges with the very being of the body. As we have seen, to be a body is to be tied to a certain world, and our body is not primarily *in* space, but rather is *of* space.**
> 
> (Merleau-Ponty 2012: 149; emphasis added)

CHAPTER 3

# Expressive form

## Since feeling is first

Having begun by suggesting that *the body* is the focus of Merleau-Ponty's philosophy, in the previous chapter it should have become clear that this is actually a somewhat misleading statement. In fact, it is more accurate to say that *embodiment* is the central theme, including those shared qualities of materiality and volume that are common to both bodies and material things. The peculiar characteristic of human embodiment is that it gives rise to a particular form of consciousness, but we should also bear in mind that most of the other bodies in the world may also possess this quality, even in some minimal form. Evolution teaches us that complex organisms have emerged gradually from simpler ones, and that brains are – in relative terms – a fairly recent enhancement. In fact, only organisms that need to move around in the world have actually bothered to develop them. A curious reversal that nicely illustrates this principle is the case of the humble sea squirt, a creature that uses its brain to locate a permanent nesting place and then, once settled, quickly consumes it for its own sustenance.

On the shorter time scale of so-called 'ontogenetic' development (the lifetime of the individual person) we also saw how consciousness is an emergent phenomenon. Merleau-Ponty's substantial work in child psychology demonstrates his keen interest in understanding how this happens (Merleau-Ponty 2010). A key aspect we have touched on already is the emergence of individuality, a consequence of the gradual disaggregation of self and other that begins in the first few days and weeks of life. Part of this process depends on a similar separation of the self from other material objects, a process that we saw is effectively re-enacted moment to moment each time we open our eyes on the world. One of the basic principles of Gestalt psychology by which Merleau-Ponty was strongly influenced is the idea that we perceive objects as distinct wholes, and not as collections of separate 'sense data'. In other words, we do not first perceive individual qualities which we then have to synthesize by an intellectual act. Rather, in order to perceive qualities we first have to perceive objects, using a skill that develops as the result of experience, rather than being something we are born with, as is often assumed.

**We do not first perceive individual qualities which we then have to synthesize by an intellectual act. Rather, in order to perceive qualities we first have to perceive objects, using a skill that develops as the result of experience.**

### Learning to see

The so-called figure–ground structure of perception – which means that objects are always seen as standing out against a background – is perhaps best illustrated by a simple example: for instance, the famous optical illusion of two faces in silhouette. We can read this in two ways of course, but not both at the same time: it is either seen as a white goblet against a black background, or two faces in profile with a white space between. The other crucial aspect of the way in which things appear to us as *gestalts* or structured wholes, is the fact that an object's qualities seem to be bound together so that one reinforces another. In one of Merleau-Ponty's radio broadcasts on the theme of *The World of Perception* he quoted with approval one of Sartre's descriptions that nicely captures this phenomenon: 'It is the sourness of the lemon which is yellow; it is the yellow of the lemon which is sour' (Merleau-Ponty 2008: 62). As we saw in Chapter 2 Merleau-Ponty often explained a general principle by referring to what would usually be classed as a pathological problem – in this case, the sensory confusion experienced by people who suffer from synaesthesia. This relatively common condition involves 'hearing colours' or 'seeing sounds', and is caused by a crossover of neural pathways that feed sensory information to the brain. Merleau-Ponty took this abnormality as paradigmatic for all perception, as he was keen to demonstrate that sensory qualities are always experienced in combination:

> We see the rigidity and the fragility of the glass and, when it breaks with a crystal-clear sound, this sound is borne by the visible glass. We see the elasticity of steel, the ductility of molten steel, the hardness of the blade in a plane, and the softness of its shavings. The form of objects is not their geometrical shape: ... it speaks to all of our senses at the same time as it speaks to vision.
>
> (Merleau-Ponty 2012: 238)

The relationship of visual and tactile sensations was already a theme in philosophy prior to Merleau-Ponty. It appeared within the eighteenth-century Empiricist tradition thanks to the earlier writings of John Locke, specifically his exchange of letters with William Molyneux on what became known as the 'Molyneux Problem'. The question posed was whether someone who had been blind from birth but later had their sight restored would be able to recognize objects visually that they had only previously known by touch. While the Empiricists would answer in the negative, as they saw the senses functioning independently, Merleau-Ponty's approach would allow us to answer yes, even if not all recent commentators agree (Gallagher 2005: 163). More recent experiments in psychology would also support this positive conclusion, such as where babies have been shown to prefer looking at pictures of dummies that they only know by the sense of touch (Gallagher 2005: 160).

Even more significant for the way in which we construct our broader sense of three-dimensional space is the intermodal connection between vision and proprioception that develops as we learn to move our whole body around in the world. Merleau-Ponty explained this relationship by referring to another case study from clinical research; this time an experiment performed by the psychologist George Malcolm Stratton. Stratton's experiment involved wearing a pair of inverting prismatic glasses which turned his view of the world upside-down. This is technically a 'correction' of what happens in normal vision, in the sense that the image on the back of the retina is normally already inverted. At first, he reported confusion as his vision seemed to contradict the experience of his body, but after a few days of practice with the glasses what he saw was gradually 'corrected' – his brain was able to normalize the image by re-inverting back to normal. This correction worked effectively only for more distant views, but not so well when he looked at his own body, and even tended to flip back again momentarily when he reached out to pick things up. In these situations he reported confusion and a sense of disorientation as he was unable to reconcile the contradictory information received from visual and bodily feedback. A further study by Max Wertheimer that Merleau-Ponty also described involved wearing mirror glasses that tilted the image to around 45 degrees from the vertical. To begin with the participant had to lean sideways in order to make sense of the view, but after a few minutes moving around inside a room the view was again gradually corrected. In both cases it seemed that bodily feedback was effectively overriding the visual information which the brain was then able to adjust, resolving the contradiction between them and reconstructing a consistent experience.

While there may be some inconsistencies in Merleau-Ponty's account of the Stratton experiment, there is good evidence in both these cases to support the link between vision and action. More recent evidence can also be found in cases of sensory substitution, such as the 'tactile vision' apparatus devised in the 1970s by the neuroscientist Paul Bach-y-Rita (Clark 2003: 125f). The basic principle of Bach-y-Rita's system is that it transforms visual information into tactile signals, by converting a pixelated video-camera image into a grid of vibrating pins. A blind person wearing a head-mounted camera, coupled with the grid of pins held in contact with the skin, can then receive visual data as a pattern of vibrations which they can learn to interpret as basic visual images.

**While there may be some inconsistencies in Merleau-Ponty's account of the Stratton experiment, there is good evidence in both these cases to support the link between vision and action.**

Much recent writing on the theme of touch has questioned the traditional dominance of vision, and likewise, as we have seen already in Chapter 1, for Merleau-Ponty tactile experience was the paradigm for all perception (Classen 2005; Pallasmaa 2005). The key idea that touch has a spatial dimension is illustrated by examples of blind people whose sight has been restored. These cases show that visual perceptions are gradually integrated into a spatial framework that previous bodily experiences have already set in place. Acoustic sensations likewise give us a strong sense of orientation, and a blind person tapping a cane on the ground will sense the size and shape of a space from listening to the changing sounds. Merleau-Ponty also moved beyond this to suggest that music can alter our sense of space, and in one of his more colourful passages he described the experience of sitting in a concert hall as the music is about to begin:

> **Music erodes visible space, surrounds it, and causes it to shift, such that these overdressed listeners – who take on a judgmental air and exchange comments or smirks without noticing that the ground begins to tremble beneath them – are soon like a ship's crew tossed about on the surface of a stormy sea.**
>
> (Merleau-Ponty 2012: 234)

On a more basic level, one further illustration of the vital connection between perception and action comes from a study carried out in the 1960s by two American experimental psychologists (Held and Hein 1963). The experiment involved two kittens just a few days old, at a time when their brains were developing rapidly; neural networks were being formed in response to their accumulating experience of movement. They were both enclosed in an apparatus but only one of the kittens could control its own movements; the other was attached to a harness and suspended above the ground. The second kitten was therefore carried around according to the movements of the first, so its visual information was changing even though it was not able to initiate any movement. As the first kitten could move around normally its visual perceptions changed in the usual way: its brain was able to match vision with proprioception and the normal neural circuits could develop. The second kitten had no control over its own body and its brain therefore failed to make this same connection, so when the kittens were released after a few days in the apparatus they exhibited very different kinds of behaviour. The first one could move around quite normally, but the second behaved as if it had lost its sight, bumping into barriers or stepping off edges and exhibiting a form of 'experiential blindness'. While the kitten's eyes were working perfectly well, its brain had temporarily lost a vital neural connection: it had not retained the capacity to match up its bodily movements with the incoming changes in visual information. The key issue is that normal development involves a coupling together of visual and bodily information, where the brain interprets changing visual perceptions in relation to bodily movement. This is a key part of what enables any complex organism to navigate effectively in three-dimensional space, which, thankfully, even the kittens were able to do after a few days of normal experience following their release from the experimental apparatus.

## The thickness of time and the depth of space

The general principle behind the kitten experiment is that perception is a consequence of action, and in a sense, therefore, we could also say that action is a consequence of perception. Merleau-Ponty was particularly interested in the temporal aspect of this circular relation; the way in which the ability to perceive a meaningful world gradually emerges from bodily engagement over time. The model of time that he used to explain this process was adopted from Edmund Husserl, who had already suggested that our common-sense idea of the present moment as an isolated instant is actually a misleading convention. In fact, it is more correct to think of it as a composite of so-called 'retentions' and 'protentions': the gradual fading of the moment just passed overlaid by anticipations of the one about to come (Merleau-Ponty 2012: 439–442). Rather than conscious memories or explicit projections which would take too long to bring 'online', these moments of past and future perception are intrinsic parts of the here and now; vital components of the sense of continuity and flow that is characteristic of embodied experience.

# Moments of past and future perception are intrinsic parts of the here and now; vital components of the sense of continuity and flow that is characteristic of embodied experience.

Another aspect of perception that Merleau-Ponty took from Husserl was the idea that objects are revealed to us gradually in partial views. Husserl called these *Abschattungen*, usually translated as adumbrations or foreshadowings, meaning sketchy or incomplete outlines of things that compel us to explore them further. The curiosity to confirm that these outlines actually do belong to three-dimensional entities is part of what Merleau-Ponty described as our response to the solicitations of the world. What we discover in exploring the world – using our perceptual abilities like vision and touch – is a field of independent objects seen against a background of other objects, in what Merleau-Ponty called a two-part 'horizonal' structure. Part of this structure is the 'outer horizon' that was described by Gestalt psychologists: the background against which an object that we are currently focusing on can be seen to be standing out. The other is the more complex phenomenon that Merleau-Ponty called the 'inner horizon', which helps to explain how we can perceive the whole of an object when only the part currently facing us is actually visible. The basic idea is that objects have hidden sides that we assume are there even when we cannot see them, because experience has taught us that we could see them if we walked around behind them and had a look. This is a tendency that theatre and film-set designers have known about for a long time, as even painted scenery can achieve an illusion of reality when the audience's viewpoint is carefully restricted. The key thing to appreciate is the give-and-take aspect of this process of horizonal perception: it is precisely because objects partially conceal themselves from us that they are able to appear to us as objects at all. Likewise, in the 'outer horizonal' or figure–background relationship, our sense of the background as continuing behind the object relies on its ability to at least momentarily obscure the other objects from us. This is particularly the case in our perception of spaces within cities, where this structure operates at a number of different levels: from 'object buildings' like churches and museums, which stand out against the background of more everyday architecture, to those significant individual ceremonial spaces which might also be expressed as distinct 'objects'.

For Merleau-Ponty, the natural curiosity that draws us in to explore an object further – to confirm our initial assumptions about its three-dimensional qualities – might tempt us to think that there is an end to this process once we have exhaustively investigated all its previously hidden aspects. In fact, this is an endless process because we can never grasp the object *in itself*; even if we could see it from an infinite number of viewpoints there would still be more to explore: 'For example, I see the neighbouring house from a particular angle. It would be seen differently from the right bank of the Seine, from the inside of the house, and differently still from an airplane. Not one of these appearances is the house *itself*' (Merleau-Ponty 2012: 69). 'The house has its water pipes, its foundation, and perhaps its cracks growing secretly in the thickness of the ceilings. We never see them, but it has them, together with its windows or chimneys that are visible for us' (Merleau-Ponty 2012: 72). The fact that Merleau-Ponty used the example of a house is significant for a number of reasons, one of which being his notion that to see any object is to 'come to inhabit it and to thereby grasp all things according to the sides these other things turn toward this object' (Merleau-Ponty 2012: 71). In other words, when we are focusing on the visible faces that an object currently has turned towards us, he claimed that the other objects act as witnesses for the views that we cannot ourselves at that moment see:

> When I see the lamp on my table, I attribute to it not merely the qualities that are visible from my location, but also those that the fireplace, the table and the walls can 'see'. The back of my lamp is merely the face that it 'shows' to the fireplace.
>
> (Merleau-Ponty 2012: 71)

Merleau-Ponty seems to be proposing something slightly mystical in this suggestion that objects can 'see' each other, but as we will see in Chapter 4 it is also a principle that he found in the work of visual artists like Paul Cézanne. The key thing to note for now is that this 'horizontal' structure of perception is based on our sense of depth: a consequence of our learning to experience objects as we move our bodies in the space between them. This should also remind us that the double structure of horizons also has a temporal dimension, in terms of the layering of retentions and protentions that gradually accumulate in our experience. Hence Merleau-Ponty's claim that depth is the 'most existential of all dimensions' in the sense that our history of previous experiences of objects is what ultimately locates us in space:

> **My body is geared into the world when my perception provides me with the most varied and the most clearly articulated spectacle possible, and when my motor intentions, as they unfold, receive the responses they anticipate from the world. This maximum of clarity in perception and action specifies a perceptual *ground*, a background for my life, a general milieu for the coexistence of my body and the world.**
>
> (Merleau-Ponty 2012: 261)

In other words it is this unfolding bodily process that anchors us in space and time, as opposed to being detached observers gazing at two-dimensional screens. One illustration of this principle of immersion is the comparison of Renaissance and Cubist paintings, where the former relies on an idealized observer located at the vanishing point of the perspective grid. The latter, however, suggests a moving observer embedded within the space of the painting itself, with multiple viewpoints represented simultaneously, as if the viewing time had been magically compressed.

## This 'horizontal' structure of perception is based on our sense of depth, a consequence of our learning to experience objects as we move our bodies in the space between them.

Other examples from art and architecture illustrate the vital role of bodily exploration, showing how visual perception can be manipulated and optical illusions easily created. The American artist James Turrell's famous sky-viewing rooms rework the traditional technique of creating framed views of the distant landscape. Visitors enter what looks like an internal space that actually turns out to have an open roof, with its unglazed skylight detailed in a way that conceals the thickness of the roof construction. This picture-frame effect dramatically flattens the view of the sky into a blue plane at ceiling level (Turrell et al. 1999: 96–101). This effect was also explored in Turrell's gallery-based work involving framed views from one space into another, where a visual illusion is created that oscillates between flatness and depth. What at first looks like a two-dimensional image on a wall is also a window opening into an apparently infinite space, and as the viewer is prevented from entering this space there is no way of resolving this curious ambiguity (Turrell et al. 1999: 102–121).

Historical examples of this framing and flattening effect can be found in many different cultures, though perhaps the most interesting and most imitated examples are the so-called 'scholar gardens' of Suzhou in China. The Chinese designers were also inspired by their long tradition of landscape painting, which partly explains their interest in playing up the ambiguity of image and reality. The compact arrangement of walled gardens, each with framed views from one to the next, has the effect of rendering the three-dimensional landscape as a series of overlapping two-dimensional images. As the visitor follows a meandering route around the garden, these confusions are alternately resolved and then reinstated: one garden is revealed as a three-dimensional space, while the previous one is apparently flattened back into a painted scene. For the viewer this can be both an exhilarating and a disorientating experience – something that the Icelandic artist Olafur Eliasson has explored to great effect in a recent video work. In *Your Embodied Garden* from 2013 the artist created a series of mini-performances within two of the Suzhou gardens, combining the movements of a single dancer and a circular mirror to playfully exaggerate these spatial ambiguities (Eliasson 2013).

One lesson from all these examples relates to what Merleau-Ponty referred to as the solicitations of the world; the idea that we are drawn into a bodily engagement as we seek resolution of perceptual uncertainties. In architectural terms this can also be related to those spaces that seem to call out for bodily movement, particularly those that depart from the conventions of 'classical' perspectival space. By defying the obvious logic of linear axes and symmetrical layouts that could be quickly grasped in a single view, there is an important strand of modernist architecture that began to explore new forms of spatial organization. Good examples of this can be found in the work of the German architect Hans Scharoun whose use of free-flowing spaces and fragmented geometries are often described as inviting exploration. In his Berlin Philharmonie (1963), perhaps his most significant built project, the foyer space is structured around 'staircases [that] demand exploration', according to the historian Peter Blundell Jones in a recent book on *Architecture and Movement* (Blundell Jones and Meagher 2015: 15).

Steven Holl, an architect who makes frequent reference to Merleau-Ponty, also describes this experience of movement as a key influence on his design approach:

> **The movement of the body as it crosses through overlapping perspectives formed within spaces is the elemental connection between ourselves and architecture ... Our faculty of judgement is incomplete without this experience of crossing through spaces, the turn and twist of the body engaging a long and then a short perspective, an up-and-down movement, an open-and-closed or dark-and-light rhythm of geometries – these are the core of the spatial score of architecture.**
>
> **(Holl 2000: 26)**

## The bodily form of things

So far we have been focusing on the body as the medium of our experience, and how our knowledge of the world is grounded in our bodily ability to engage with it, by deploying a set of skills that are both socially and biologically structured, owing to our having acquired them while growing up in a shared cultural environment. While we might be tempted to think of the body as our first 'technical object' – as the French anthropologist Marcel Mauss claimed in 1935 (Mauss 2006: 83) – we saw in Chapter 2 how this idea has recently been turned around. Evolutionary theory now suggests that it was actually early technology that gave us the ability to begin thinking of the body in this way. In effect, we began to see ourselves reflected back in the forms of the objects that we ourselves had created.

## Knowledge of the world is grounded in our bodily ability to engage with it, by deploying a set of skills that are both socially and biologically structured.

There is therefore a long history to the idea that consciousness begins with embodiment, and an important element of this process is the way in which we 'read' the world in bodily terms. This comes about partly through our ontogenetic history and the fact that the very first 'objects' we encounter are other human bodies. One consequence of this is that the body becomes a kind of framework for all perception, and it is this idea that Merleau-Ponty was also keen to explore:

> So the way we relate to the things of the world is no longer as a pure intellect trying to master an object or space that stands before it. Rather, this relationship is an ambiguous one, between beings who are both embodied and limited and an enigmatic world of which we catch a glimpse (indeed which we haunt incessantly) but only ever from points of view that hide as much as they reveal, a world in which every object displays the human face it acquires in a human gaze.
>
> (Merleau-Ponty 2004: 69f)

So, in addition to reading the world in terms of the opportunities it offers for action, Merleau-Ponty also claimed that we have an emotional response to the style or manner in which opportunities are offered. This qualitative aspect is a reaction to what he called the 'physiognomy' of things; that characteristic gestural quality that all forms seem to present to us. In his work on child psychology he suggested that the recognition of bodily gestures is one of the earliest abilities that humans develop and, as we now know, this begins with the newborn baby's emotional connection with the face of the mother (Gopnik et al. 2001: 27–31). Later in the same essay Merleau-Ponty referred to other studies of behaviour, noting that children begin to imitate the gestures and actions of other people from around the age of three. He suggested that the re-enactment of certain gestures becomes a means of internalizing and thereby understanding them, basing his argument on Henri Wallon's idea of 'postural impregnation'. He also referred to the continuation of this imitative behaviour into adulthood, through an amusing example that also highlights the anticipatory aspect of this tendency:

> **In sum, our perceptions arouse in us a reorganization of motor conduct, without our already having learned the gestures in question. We know the famous example of the spectators at a football game who make the proper gesture at the moment when the player would make it.**
>
> **(Merleau-Ponty 1964a: 145)**

This notion of a fundamental continuity between seeing and doing has also been confirmed by recent research in neuroscience, specifically by the discovery of the so-called 'mirror neuron' system, first described by Vittorio Gallese and his colleagues from the University of Parma, in Italy. The basic principle is that the neural circuits involved in the production of bodily movement are also active during the observation of movement in other people. In other words, when we are watching someone performing a particular action we are activating the same neural network that controls our own performance of the same action (Gallese et al. 1996). The neuroscientist V. S. Ramachandran has even called them 'Gandhi neurons' as they appear to play a vital role in creating empathic connections between people (Ramachandran 2013). Recent experiments have also demonstrated differences in the levels of activation according to the familiarity of the observer with the actions they are observing. This is somewhat contrary to what Merleau-Ponty implied in the example of the spectators just quoted because, in fact, the mirror neuron circuits do respond much more strongly when, for example, highly skilled performers such as dancers are watching routines in which they themselves are specifically trained (Calvo-Merino et al. 2006).

The mirror neuron system allows us to 'read' other people's actions by simulating or inwardly performing them, rather as in moments of concentrated reading when we find ourselves whispering the printed words. It also suggests that perception involves a kind of rehearsal for action, which also fits the evidence of an evolutionary link between increasing motor and perceptual abilities. As Merleau-Ponty had already proposed:

> ... there is, as a result, a necessity for acknowledging that the body has a capacity for 'meditation', for the 'inward formulation' of gestures. I see unfolding the different phases of the process, and this perception is of such a nature as to arouse in me the preparation of a motor activity related to it. It is this fundamental correspondence between perception and motility – the power of perception to organize a motor conduct that Gestalt theorists have insisted on.
>
> (Merleau-Ponty 1964a: 146)

Another aspect of the evolutionary dimension of this connection between perception and action is the adaptive role of emotional recognition in providing vital information for survival. Perceived threats from other animals invoke a so-called 'fight or flight' response – a combination of instinctive and acquired behaviour – and this is partly based on the ability to discern when a vague threat may be turning into an attack. In a more nuanced way this kind of emotional signalling also happens among the members of a social group, where the ability to recognize the emotional states of others provides a kind of pre-linguistic form of communication (Corballis 2002: 25–30). When sound is also used to reinforce bodily gesture this can further increase the survival benefit, as demonstrated in the well-documented case of the chimpanzee 'alarm call', which quickly alerts a whole group to the approach of a potential predator.

## The mirror neuron system allows us to 'read' other people's actions by simulating or inwardly performing them, rather as in moments of concentrated reading when we find ourselves whispering the printed words.

All of this suggests that the recognition of emotions develops very early, in both an evolutionary and an individual sense, and this has recently led the philosopher Jesse Prinz to propose that we should consider emotions themselves *as* perceptions. While this claim is still open to argument among philosophers – based partly on questions of terminology – Prinz himself makes a powerful case for the primacy of our 'gut reactions' to things. By focusing on the emotional component of this initial process of 'embodied appraisal', he helps to explain what we have described above as the integration of perception and action (Prinz 2004). As Merleau-Ponty himself has suggested in relation to emotional expressions, gestures provide another illustration of the underlying principle of 'reversibility':

> **Consider an angry or threatening gesture ... I do not perceive the anger or the threat as a psychological fact hidden behind the gesture, I read the anger in the gesture. The gesture does not make me think of anger, it is the anger itself. ... Everything happens as if the other person's intention inhabited my body, or as if my intentions inhabited his body ... I confirm the other person and the other person confirms me.**
>
> (Merleau-Ponty 2012: 190f)

There is a suggestion here that 'acting out' an expression can itself actually bring about the emotion; a curious phenomenon that had been previously noted as far back as the eighteenth century. The American psychologist William James, writing in 1890, claimed: 'Everyone knows how panic is increased by flight, and how the giving way to the symptoms of grief or anger increases those passions themselves' (James 1950: 462). James then goes on to quote Edmund Burke, who is himself quoting the Renaissance philosopher Tommaso Campanella, describing how the evidence of outward expressions allows us to sense what others are thinking (James 1950: 464). Merleau-Ponty himself provided a novel example of this influence of action upon mental states, in explaining how we 'call forth sleep' by adopting the posture and behaviour of the sleeper (Merleau-Ponty 2012: 219). Psychologists today who are exploring the implications of the mirror neuron system have brought together several of these themes under the banner of 'simulation theory'. Rather than having an explicit 'theory of mind', which we apply in order to decode someone else's intentions, the new theory suggests we can instead grasp them intuitively by inwardly replicating their behaviour (Gallese and Goldman 1998).

Merleau-Ponty also felt that this reciprocity in the gestural communication between people was the basis of our emotional response to the appearance of physical objects. He described this in his later work as the body's 'motor echo' of the world; a visceral and bodily reaction to the physiognomy or shape of things (Merleau-Ponty 1968: 144). He also used the example of the 'atmosphere' of a city to show how much of our initial grasp of a thing is based on this broad sense of its overall style or manner of being:

> For me, Paris is not a thousand-sided object or a collection of perceptions. Just as a human being manifests the same affective essence in his hand gestures, his gait, and the sound of his voice, each explicit perception in my journey through Paris – the cafés, the faces, the poplars along the quays, the bends of the Seine – is cut out of the total being of Paris, and only serves to confirm a certain style or a certain sense. And when I arrived there for the first time, the first streets that I saw upon leaving the train station were – like the first words of a stranger – only manifestations of a still ambiguous, though already incomparable essence. In fact, we hardly perceive any objects

at all, just as we do not see the eyes of a familiar face, but rather its gaze and its expression.

(Merleau-Ponty 2012: 294)

<u>This reciprocity in the gestural communication between people was the basis of our emotional response to the appearance of physical objects. He described this in his later work as the body's 'motor echo' of the world; a visceral and bodily reaction to the physiognomy of things.</u>

### Architecture of empathy

The suggestion that we do not first perceive an object of a certain geometric shape or material, but rather that we begin with a more global sense of its character, is expressed in this notion of a bodily physiognomy. We might find support for this view in nineteenth-century aesthetics, specifically in the concept of empathy as explored by a number of German writers. The term itself is translated from *Einfühlung*, meaning literally 'feeling in', and relates to the bodily response of the viewer when experiencing an artwork. Empathic responses can be triggered by both figurative and abstract images. For example, alongside the explicit emotions of the people depicted in a painting, there is also a gestural quality in the way that the artist has applied the paint. It is this more abstract level of gestural communication that Le Corbusier was also referring to in this famous passage from *Toward an Architecture*, first published in 1923:

> My house is practical. Thank you, as I thank the engineers of the railroad and the telephone company. You have not touched my heart.
> But the walls rise against the sky in an order such that I am moved. I sense your intentions. You were gentle, brutal, charming or dignified. Your

> stones tell me so. ... They are the language of architecture. With inert materials, based on a more or less utilitarian program that you *go beyond*, you have established relationships that moved me. It is architecture.
>
> (Le Corbusier 2008: 233)

The ability to be 'moved by' an experience has its roots in our ability to move, which gives us a kind of inward knowledge of what it feels like to move in the way that a form suggests. This may be a large-scale dynamic effect within an overall composition – as suggested already in the work of Hans Scharoun and Steven Holl – or it may be the more intimate sense of movement implied at the level of construction details, in the assembly of building components or the traces of tool marks in a surface. We will return in Chapter 4 to consider this more intimate theme of materiality, but for now it is important to appreciate how they are both grounded in embodiment. Returning to the theme of empathy, as developed by the art historian Heinrich Wölfflin in 1886, we find a clear statement of the link between aesthetics and bodily experience:

> Physical forms possess a character only because we ourselves possess a body. If we were purely visual beings, we would always be denied an aesthetic judgment of the physical world. But as human beings with a body that teaches us the nature of gravity, contraction, strength, and so on, we gather the experience that enables us to identify with the conditions of other forms ... We have carried loads and experienced pressure and counterpressure ... and that is why we can appreciate the noble serenity of a column and understand the tendency of all matter to spread out formlessly on the ground.
>
> (Wölfflin 1994: 151)

The architectural historian David Leatherbarrow describes this as a defining quality of Baroque architecture, a kind of tension or balance of opposing forces that expresses movement as if frozen in time. In discussing the Lewis Glucksman Gallery in Cork by the architects O'Donnell + Tuomey, he draws attention to the formal arrangement of spiralling volumes that expresses just this sense of movement. He relates the tension between the overlapping elevated galleries to the Baroque principle of *contrapposto*. This was often used by painters and sculptors in depicting human figures as if frozen in the middle of a twisting or turning movement. The typical pose involves the feet, hips, head and torso all rotating slightly in different directions at once, resulting in a powerful sense of suspended animation that evokes a similar tension within the viewer (Leatherbarrow 2009: 234–236).

It is not just in architecture that these bodily analogies still echo, as our language is also laden with anthropomorphic references. The eighteenth-century Neapolitan philosopher Giambattista Vico was perhaps the first to note the anatomical references in the way we describe the landscape. In Book II of his *New Science* on the theme of 'Poetic Logic' he quoted many typical examples: from the 'head' of a mountain to the 'foot' of a cliff; and from the 'brow' of a hill, a narrow 'neck' of land to the 'gorge' of a river. Even with household objects this connection continues, from the 'lip' of a cup to the 'teeth' of a comb, and from the 'tongue' of a shoe to the 'hands' of a clock (Vico 1984: 129). The American philosophers Lakoff and Johnson have extended these observations further, developing a more general analysis of the bodily metaphors underlying our everyday patterns of thought (Lakoff and Johnson 1980).

They describe the basic structure of human embodiment as the source of our spatial orientation, from the fact that we stand upright and face forwards with a strong sense of left and right. This also translates into a temporal system in the sense that the future is 'in front' of us and the past 'behind'. The fact that we have to expend effort to keep ourselves upright against the downward force of gravity has led us to assign a positive value to things that are higher, and a negative one to those that are lower. They also contend that even logical principles can be derived from physical models, such as the habit of defining and classifying objects which is based on the primary metaphor of containment. For example, the principle of syllogism, first proposed by Aristotle, is based on the principle that if an object is inside one container that is then placed inside another, then the object must, by definition, also be inside the second. For instance: all men are mortal; Socrates is a man; therefore Socrates is mortal.

O'Donnell + Tuomey Architects, Lewis Glucksman Gallery, Cork, 2004.

Lakoff and Johnson also make some interesting links between reasoning and architecture, in the sense that our philosophical 'edifice' must be 'built' on the strongest 'foundations' or it risks being 'demolished' in a debate and perhaps left in 'ruins' (Lakoff and Johnson 1980). This is a familiar metaphor throughout the history of philosophy with its habit of erecting grandiose intellectual 'systems', albeit one of which Merleau-Ponty himself was profoundly suspicious.

Even logical principles can be derived from physical models, such as the habit of defining and classifying objects which is based on the primary metaphor of containment.

Merleau-Ponty was also acutely aware of this sense of bodily orientation, and in particular how it forms the basis of our understanding of prepositions like 'on', 'in' and 'above':

> But what sense could the word 'on' have for a subject who could not be situated by his body in front of the world? It implies a distinction between up and down, that is, an 'oriented space'. When I say that an object is on a table, I always place myself (in thought) in the table or the object, and I apply a category to them that in principle fits the relation between my body and external objects.
>
> (Merleau-Ponty 2012: 103)

This idea that we 'feel ourselves into' an object, in this bodily sense – much as the concept of empathy implies – perhaps also goes some way to explaining the historical link between architecture and the body. Since at least the time when Vitruvius wrote his book *De Architectura* in the first century AD, the idea of the building as a body has been a persistent metaphor. It enjoyed a major revival during the Renaissance thanks to the work of L. B. Alberti and others, as the architectural historian Joseph Rykwert has demonstrated so convincingly (Rykwert 1996). This was based on the theological notion of an underlying 'universal harmony'; the idea that all natural forms are proportioned according to strict mathematical ratios, from the revolution of the planets to the spiral of a snail shell. As with musical composition, so with bodies and buildings – any departure from these divinely inspired rules will surely lead to discord. In the seventeenth and eighteenth centuries mathematics underwent a gradual secularization, becoming instead predominantly a tool of the industrial and scientific revolution (Pérez-Gómez 1983). Despite this, in the twentieth century the building-as-body metaphor has once again resurfaced, perhaps most notably in the work of Le Corbusier, including in his proportioning system known as *The Modulor* (Le Corbusier 1951).

In the mid-1960s when phenomenology first had an impact in architecture, again it was the body that became the primary area of interest. This time two alternative trends could be identified: alongside the traditional focus on the experienced object, attention now shifted towards the experiencing subject – the effects that the building has on the body itself. While postmodernism tends to be associated with the revival of the former – through architects such as Michael Graves' use of explicitly figurative references – there is also, for example in the work of Charles Moore, a sense that postmodernism was equally concerned with the impact on the building user (Bloomer et al. 1977). It is also now clear that Moore's ideas were directly inspired by phenomenological sources, despite the fact that the rise of postmodernism has traditionally been linked with the influence of semiotics and structuralism (Otero-Pailos 2010). In the visual arts in the same period Merleau-Ponty's influence was more direct and explicit, on both artists and critics concerned with the experience of Minimalist painting and sculpture (Potts 2000: 207–234). In architecture this impact took much longer to develop, partly due to the dominance of the work of Martin Heidegger. Interestingly, there is another overlap in relation to one of Merleau-Ponty's key sources, in the take-up of Gestalt psychology in architectural theory in the 1960s. Notable examples include the early writings of Christian Norberg-Schulz, as well as the similarly inspired work of the German theorist Rudolf Arnheim, which focused specifically on perception in the experience of art and architecture (Norberg-Schulz 1966; Arnheim 1977).

It is also now clear that Moore's ideas were directly inspired by phenomenological sources, despite that the fact that the rise of postmodernism has traditionally been linked with the influence of semiotics and structuralism.

In this chapter I have shown that there are at least three senses in which architecture and the body may be related. Beyond the historical persistence of the idea of a 'universal harmony' linking the proportions of all bodies – human or otherwise – there is the metaphorical idea that the 'building is a body', in the sense that we project ourselves into an expressive composition of forms by some kind of empathic process of 'feeling in'. At the same time there is also the idea that we experience the world not so much *as* a building but rather *through* it. This is when – as with a prosthetic extension – the building becomes a means of reaching out to experience the world in a new way, beyond the limits of our biological bodies. In Chapter 4 we look at this process in more detail, to ask whether we are reaching back to recover a lost connection with the world, or whether, as implied already, this state of continuity is where we actually begin.

The final word in this chapter goes to the French neuroscientist Alain Berthoz, writing in 1997 on *The Brain's Sense of Movement*, who turns his attention to the role of the built environment in stimulating – or otherwise – the body's sensory engagement:

> Perception, which is simulated action, needs to find natural or artificial objects in the environment that imply action. So our brains take pleasure in playing, in guessing the real and the false, in lying, in laughing and crying, in capturing and fleeing, in predicting the future – in a word, living. The architects of the Grande Bibliothèque, of the Opéra Bastille, of Beaubourg tried above all to arrange people and things in an orderly way, but ... they

condemned us to boredom. I accuse them of the crime of melancholy, of leading millions of people to despair, of crimes against the biological brain – its flexibility, its desire for movement and variation.

(Berthoz 2000: 256f)

CHAPTER 4

# Tectonics and materials

## The flesh of the world

Several writers have claimed that there was a fundamental shift in the direction of Merleau-Ponty's later work. On the one hand, there were many themes that recurred throughout his writings, and we have looked at some of these in Chapters 2 and 3. On the other hand, in his final decade of work some differences began to appear, in both a more elaborate – one might even say poetic – style of writing, as well as in the content itself. In the early writings, as we have seen already, Merleau-Ponty drew substantially from scientific evidence, from neurological experiments and case studies from which he developed a new understanding of perception. On the foundation provided by this early exploration beyond the confines of philosophy he began to apply his new conceptual framework, producing separate studies of distinct areas of activity such as art, language and literature. The collection of essays translated as *Signs*, originally released in 1960, gives a clear sense of this later direction. It was the last book he was able to see published before his untimely death in the following year. Alongside the political writing on contemporary issues that he continued to produce throughout his career, his other essays show a growing interest in the creative output of artists and writers: work that he felt held its own kind of philosophical significance.

### Dualism redoubled?

We will look in detail at some of these later writings in both this and Chapter 5. For now, there is one more thing worth noting about the overall direction of Merleau-Ponty's career, and this is what he himself wrote about it in a critical reflection on his early work. In an essay presented as part of his application for the Chair in Philosophy at the Collège de France, he described what he saw as the overall aim of his philosophy:

> I have tried first of all to re-establish the roots of the mind in its body and in its world, going against doctrines which treat perception as a simple result of the action of external things on our body as well as against those which insist on the autonomy of consciousness. These philosophies commonly forget ... the insertion of the mind in corporeality, the ambiguous relation which we entertain with our body and, correlatively, with perceived things.
> (Merleau-Ponty 1964a: 3f)

So far this seems like a confirmation of what we saw in Chapter 2, but later he went on to describe his then currently emerging projects. One of those he rather grandly labelled a 'theory of truth', intended to address the emergence of conceptual knowledge from the process of bodily experience. The tragedy of his early death meant that he never completed this ambitious text, although his unfinished manuscript was published posthumously, along with his revisions and working notes. Some of these notes contain vital clues to the new direction of his later thought, including the questioning of one of the basic principles that guided his earlier work: 'The problems posed in *Phenomenology of Perception* are insoluble because I start there from the "consciousness"–"object" distinction' (Merleau-Ponty 1968: 200). And just a few pages before that he had stated: 'The problems that remain after this first description: they are due to the fact that in part I retained the philosophy of "consciousness"' (Merleau-Ponty 1968: 183).

What he was questioning here is the apparently binary opposition implied by the phenomenological principle known as intentionality, meaning that to be conscious is, as we have seen, necessarily to be conscious of something. It therefore appeared that phenomenology must begin with two distinct 'objects': consciousness itself; and that *thing of* which it is conscious. This separation immediately created a dilemma: how to explain the link between these entities which are apparently so different in kind – the mind and the world, in other words – or the 'thinking thing' as opposed to the 'extended thing' that Descartes had famously described (Descartes 1985: 127). For Merleau-Ponty, therefore, the consciousness–object distinction seemed to imply the reinstatement of mind–body dualism, resulting in the same problem of explaining how the two parts can be linked. In other words, a fundamental question seemed to remain unanswered in his earlier work: how is it possible for a mind to have reliable knowledge of the world?

# A fundamental question seemed to remain unanswered in his earlier work: how is it possible for a mind to have reliable knowledge of the world?

This question forms the cornerstone of what is known in philosophy as 'epistemology': the study of the nature and limits of human knowledge of the world, as opposed to the world as such. Philosophy that deals with the latter is usually referred to as 'ontology'; literally the 'study of being' or the nature of things in themselves. Even among contemporary philosophers there are arguments about which category phenomenology belongs to, as it seems that all of the key figures – including Merleau-Ponty – were, in fact, working across both areas. It is fair to say that there was a shift of emphasis in Merleau-Ponty's later work as he widened the scope of his investigations from his initial focus on perception. As I have suggested already in Chapters 2 and 3, Merleau-Ponty was moving towards an understanding of consciousness as the outcome rather than the origin of the process of perception. For me, this is implied already in the early writings including *Phenomenology of Perception*, but it is only in later works such as *The Visible and the Invisible* that this idea became fully explicit. A good sense of the range of views expressed by his many commentators can be seen in what are probably two of the most important landmarks in Merleau-Ponty scholarship. A translated work by the French philosopher Renaud Barbaras from 1991 proposes a definitive break between the early and the later work. By contrast, an earlier book by Gary Brent Madison provides an equally convincing unified account of a seemingly smooth and seamless development in the direction of Merleau-Ponty's thinking (Madison 1981; Barbaras 2004).

In Merleau-Ponty's final work he proposed what amounts to a new ontological category: the 'flesh of the world', out of which our understanding of all other categories emerges. This idea suggests that the everyday understanding of ourselves as experiencing subjects – distinct from the world of objects – is not where perception begins but actually where it ends. He is therefore proposing a new way of thinking about experience, where consciousness is seen as an emergent property of embodied action in the world. In other words, experience begins in a primordial state of 'con-fusion', in which what we later identify as subjects and objects are effectively 'fused together'. Prior to this abstract intellectual distinction we begin in a state of material and spatial continuity with the world. We have seen that Merleau-Ponty discussed this in a number of different contexts, such as in the movement of the body moment to moment, as we search for an 'optimal grip' on our surroundings, or in the gradual development of a child's individual identity out of what William James famously called a state of 'blooming, buzzing confusion' (James 1950/1890: 488).

We have already noted how, in Merleau-Ponty's lectures on child psychology, he had described the process by which the distinction between self and other gradually emerges. This could be seen as one of the building blocks of his later concept of the flesh, which likewise posits an ambiguous starting condition in which body and world are seen to be continuous. He proposed this idea as a means of getting around the problems created by the traditional opposition of the mental and the physical, seeing this dualistic Cartesian framework as a later intellectual overlay obscuring a more primal condition. The great philosophical dilemma of mind–body dualism was thus seen as a human-created pseudo-problem, so there should be no need to wrestle further with the mystery of how these two realms could be related to each other. It is interesting to note how this insight has been developed by some of Merleau-Ponty's successors, including, within the French tradition, Jacques Derrida and Gilles Deleuze. It also forms the conceptual basis of Bruno Latour's so-called 'actor–network theory', which describes technical systems as complex hybrids of 'nature–culture' involving human and non-human 'actors' (Latour 1993). In Merleau-Ponty's writing the concept of flesh already suggested a radical decentring of the human subject, subverting its traditionally dominant position in the history of Western philosophy. The blurring of the boundary between body and world that we have seen already in his analysis of tools also positions him – as we will see later – as an early precursor of contemporary forms of so-called 'posthumanism'.

In Merleau-Ponty's writing the concept of flesh already suggested a radical decentring of the human subject, subverting its traditionally dominant position in the history of Western philosophy.

### The reversibility of the flesh

Despite what might be assumed by the use of the word 'flesh', Merleau-Ponty was not referring here to a new kind of substance or entity. In fact, the word was meant to describe something more like a process or an attribute; an ability and a quality shared by both bodies and objects. This is another example of an idea discussed already in Chapter 2: the principle of reversibility between perceiver and perceived. If it is true that we perceive space only because we occupy space, then Merleau-Ponty likewise suggested that we perceive materiality only because we ourselves are material beings. What is shared in the concept of flesh is this quality of perceivability, which, as embodied beings, we experience from the inside by effectively 'lending our body to the world' (Merleau-Ponty 1964a: 162). This idea was also developed in more detail in the essay 'Eye and Mind', which we will look at again in Chapter 5, in relation to the process of drawing. What is curious in this text is the emphasis on the common materiality of body and world, which also recalled the earlier analysis of the extension of the body through technology:

> **Visible and mobile, my body is a thing among things; it is caught in the fabric of the world, and its cohesion is that of a thing. But because it moves itself and sees, it holds things in a circle around itself. Things are an annex**

> or prolongation of itself; they are encrusted into its flesh, they are part of its full definition; the world is made of the same stuff as the body.
>
> (Merleau-Ponty 1964a: 163)

It might appear from this description that this is what was intended by the concept of flesh; a shared mode of embodiment from which individual subjects ultimately emerge. In Chapter 5 I will try to show how this is only one part of the story, but for now I want to look more closely at the specific theme of materiality.

The final chapter of *The Visible and the Invisible*, called 'The Intertwining – The Chiasm', contains the most often cited passages of Merleau-Ponty's whole philosophy. This is especially so among those architects who have engaged directly with his ideas, for whom this essay seems to offer particular inspiration. Steven Holl, for example, refers frequently to this text, and even adapted the title for one of his own books and the name of one of his projects (Holl 1996). Formally, the Kiasma Museum consists of two distinct volumes twisting around each other, demonstrating quite literally the principle of intertwining. While there are other more subtle ways in which the architect has drawn from Merleau-Ponty's writing, at this formal level the building highlights a key philosophical dilemma. By emphasizing the merging together of two previously distinct entities it draws attention to the binary division between the body and the world, which – as we have just seen – Merleau-Ponty himself was trying to escape.

A recurring theme of Merleau-Ponty's essay 'The Intertwining – The Chiasm' is the attempt to escape from the binary model of perception which he saw as a weakness in his early work. To do this he focused on what unites the 'seer and the seen', in terms of the shared quality of perceivability that we have already hinted at above:

> When I find again the actual world such as it is, under my hands, under my eyes, up against my body, I find much more than an object: a Being of which my vision is a part, a visibility older than my operations or my acts. But this

> does not mean that there was a fusion or coinciding of me with it: on the contrary this occurs because a sort of dehiscence opens my body in two, and because between my body looked at and my body looking, my body touched and my body touching, there is overlapping or encroachment, so that we must say that the things pass into us as well as we into the things.
>
> (Merleau-Ponty 1968: 123)

Despite the suggestion that perception involves the merging of body and world, he was not claiming that we are literally absorbed back into 'primal fusion'. He was instead reminding us that each act of perception is a continuation of the body's own 'ontogenesis': the ongoing emergence of our own subjectivity (Merleau-Ponty 1968: 136). It is this accumulating history of an ongoing process that gives each of us unique identities as enduring individuals. This idea was first expressed by Merleau-Ponty towards the end of *Phenomenology of Perception*, in his discussion of the temporal aspect of subjectivity (Merleau-Ponty 2012: 450). The other element of his explanation is the principle of reversibility which also appeared in the earlier book under the heading of 'double sensations' (Merleau-Ponty 2012: 94). It is this idea that dominated his discussion in 'The Intertwining – The Chiasm,' which, as implied by the literal translation of *chiasm*, refers to a 'crossing over' between body and world in a number of different senses.

## He is not claiming that we are literally absorbed back into 'primal fusion'. He is instead reminding us that each act of perception is a continuation of the body's own 'ontogenesis': the ongoing emergence of our own subjectivity.

The more straightforward sense of reversibility can be seen most clearly in tactile experience, where the only reason we know we have touched something is because the object pushes back. Without this kind of felt or haptic feedback that comes from an object's resistance to our interference, experience would lack its characteristic texture, based on the sheer physical presence of material things. The curious aspect of this feedback process is that we tend to overlook the bodily contribution, assuming instead that when we have touched an object we have gained some information about its own qualities. Of course, what we have actually experienced is not simply the thing in itself, but rather our own bodies in the *act* of experiencing the object. This is what the philosopher David Morris called the 'crossing of body and world' which, as we saw in Chapter 2, involves an exchange of information across the interface of sensory contact (Morris 2004: 4f):

> ... this bursting forth of the mass of the body towards the things, which makes a vibration of my skin become the sleek and the rough, makes me follow with my eyes the movements and the contours of the things themselves, this magical relation, this pact between them and me according to which I lend them my body in order that they inscribe upon it and give me their resemblance ... define a vision in general and a constant style of visibility from which I cannot detach myself.
>
> (Merleau-Ponty 1968: 146)

Another way of describing this crossing over of sensory qualities is exemplified in the philosopher Nicholas Humphrey's description of the process of *Seeing Red*. He describes how, through experience, we learn to 'mislocate' sensations, by attributing our bodily stimulations to the objects that we assume to have caused them (Humphrey 2006: 62–64). In Humphrey's analysis, as for Merleau-Ponty (1968: 133–135), all perceptions are variations of touch, in the sense that all of our senses rely on some form of physical contact. Just as hearing depends on sound waves vibrating the surface of the eardrum, vision is likewise the result of light 'hitting' the back of the retina. Only in pathological cases do these sensations seem to be caused by the body itself, but in principle this conclusion is not entirely unreasonable. In normally functioning perception we rely on the fact that we have two eyes and two ears, which results in a crucial mismatch in the overlaying of information from the two 'receivers'. This allows us to locate the source of the stimulations in three-dimensional space, which we can usually confirm – as we saw earlier – by further bodily exploration.

As we have seen already, Merleau-Ponty often referred to the example of one hand touching the other, seeing it as a kind of paradigm case for all perception on the basis of this feedback principle. In 'The Intertwining' he used this to suggest a complex and metaphorical way in which bodies and objects could be described as 'reversible', in the sense that they both partake in what he called the primordial condition of visibility.

> **Between the exploration and what it will teach me, between my movements and what I touch, there must exist some relationship by principle, some kinship, according to which they are not only … vague and ephemeral deformations of the corporeal space, but the initiation to and the opening upon a tactile world. This can happen only if my hand, while it is felt from within, is also accessible from without, itself tangible, for my other hand, for example, if it takes its place among the things it touches, is in a sense one of them, opens finally upon a tangible being of which it is also a part.**
>
> (Merleau-Ponty 1968: 133)

By this he meant that objects perceive us as much as we perceive them, and that we both carry the marks of our encounters with the other (Merleau-Ponty 1968: 139). The key difference between these two histories of interaction is that, as 'minded' bodies, we have the ability to reflect on our experiences, to remember them and to learn from them, and (at least partly) assimilate them by rational means. This idea has also recently reappeared under the banner of so-called 'speculative realism', as a way of theorizing about the interaction of objects when humans are not involved. For example, the philosopher Graham Harman claims that 'fire burns cotton stupidly', suggesting that while objects can engage with certain aspects of other entities, they have a more restricted range of qualities with which they are able to interact (Harman 2011: 44f). This idea should also help us in thinking about the ongoing interactions between people and places, and the ways in which the materials we use in buildings might also be able to respond to – and then 'remember' – these encounters.

Objects perceive us as much as we perceive them, and that we both carry the marks of our encounters with the other. The key difference between these two histories of interaction is that, as 'minded' bodies, we have the ability to reflect on our experiences.

## Ideas and things

In 'Eye and Mind' Merleau-Ponty explored these ideas in the context of the visual arts, focusing especially on what artists have said and written about their experience of the process of painting. Pursuing the idea of reversibility in terms of the body as 'seen by things', he referred to the experience of the mirror image, as frequently depicted in painting:

> **Artists have often mused upon mirrors because beneath this 'mechanical trick' they recognized ... the metamorphosis of seeing and seen defines both our flesh and the painter's vocation. This explains why they have so often liked to draw themselves in the act of painting (they still do – witness Matisse's drawings), adding to what they saw then, what things saw of them.**
> 
> **(Merleau-Ponty 1964a: 168f)**

For Merleau-Ponty the mirror served as a model for the perception of all kinds of human-made things, because: 'Like all other technical objects, such as signs and tools, the mirror arises on the open circuit [that goes] from seeing body to visible body' (Merleau-Ponty 1964a: 168). In his lectures on child psychology that we have encountered already in this book, Merleau-Ponty also made reference to Jacques Lacan's influential analysis of the so-called 'mirror stage' in child development. Both thinkers see it as a pivotal moment when the child realizes 'that there can be a viewpoint taken on him', whereby 'the image of oneself makes possible the knowledge of oneself' – a key part of the gradual process of individuation by which we have all become independent subjects (Merleau-Ponty 1964a: 136). As well as the 'world seen by the artist' the painting shows the 'artist seen by the world': a 'crossing over' of the body and the medium of the paint which is recorded in the brushstrokes visible on the canvas. This idea is also echoed by the British sculptor Richard Long in describing his work as 'the portrait of myself in the world' (Long 1991: 250) and nicely captured in his early photograph of *A Line Made by Walking* (1967).

The process by which we 'read' these traces of interaction also implies the bodily involvement of the viewer, which we might now understand partly as a result of the operation of the mirror neuron system. An article from 2007, co-written by Vittorio Gallese and the art historian David Freedberg, set out to explore this possibility. They asked whether the neural circuits involved in the observation of action are also activated by viewing only the resulting traces. After scanning the brains of people while they were looking at various paintings they concluded that the same systems were, in fact, involved: 'With abstract paintings such as those by Jackson Pollock, viewers often experience a sense of bodily involvement with the movements that are implied by the physical traces – in brushmarks or paint drippings – of the creative actions of the producer of the work' (Freedberg and Gallese 2007: 197). As well as the so-called 'action paintings' by the American artist Jackson Pollock they also used the slit canvases of the Italian Lucio Fontana. In each case the viewer's response involved a kind of acting out of the artist's movement, 'reading' the work by inwardly performing the gestures that would have been involved in producing it. The writers then go on to link this idea to the nineteenth-century concept of empathy, which we looked at in Chapter 3, and a similar connection has also been suggested by Harry Francis Mallgrave in his book *The Architect's Brain* (Mallgrave 2010: 195).

## The process by which we 'read' these traces of interaction also implies the bodily involvement of the viewer, which we might now understand as partly a result of the operation of the mirror neuron system.

Richard Long, *A Line Made By Walking*, 1967.

It could be argued that it is difficult to apply these lessons to much of the art of the twentieth century, given the move towards minimalist abstraction in painting and sculpture, and an emphasis on conceptual methods. But alongside this 'crisis of the object' there has also been a growing interest in the process of viewing which, at least since the 1960s, has led to more experimental event-based – and often interactive – live performances. This point is well made by the art historian Alex Potts in his important work on *The Sculptural Imagination*, where he shows how influential Merleau-Ponty's ideas have been in the development of post-war painting and sculpture (Potts 2000: 207–234).

Merleau-Ponty was also concerned with the extent to which the drawing itself could be considered as an 'event'; for example, where the marks on the paper act as a kind of witness to the presence of another person, recording the story of their encounter with the materiality of the medium of the drawing:

> If for example I see another draw a figure, I can understand the drawing as an action because it speaks directly to my own motility. Of course the other qua author of a drawing is not yet a whole person, and there are more revealing actions than drawing – for example using language. What is essential, however, is to see that a perspective on the other is opened to me from the moment I define him and myself as 'conducts' at work in the world, as ways of 'grasping' the natural and cultural world surrounding us.
> (Merleau-Ponty 1964a: 117)

When we move from the 'tectonics of drawing' into the realm of tectonics in architecture, this notion of a narrative of bodily movement is likewise of central importance. As with the brushstrokes on the canvas that record the artist's encounter with the paint, so the surfaces of materials in buildings can also tell the story of the process of making. The saw cuts visible in timber, or the chisel marks in a block of stone, testify to a dialectical struggle between human intention and material resistance. Going beyond what Louis Kahn famously wrote about asking a brick 'what it wants to be', there is sense here of a more dynamic engagement that produces two distinct kinds of knowledge: by challenging the material we learn more about its possibilities and limitations, at the same time as understanding our own abilities – and frailties – as human beings. As John Dewey wrote in *Art as Experience*: 'Nor without resistance from surroundings would the self become aware of itself' (Dewey 1980/1934: 59).

As with the brushstrokes on the canvas that record the artist's encounter with the paint, so the surfaces of materials in buildings can also tell the story of the process of making.

### Reversible architecture

A number of recent architects and writers have focused on the importance of the material presence of buildings; specifically, how materiality and tectonic articulation invite the bodily engagement of the viewer. Kenneth Frampton, for example, in his *Studies in Tectonic Culture*, considered a number of relatively neglected designers (at least within the canon of mainstream modernist architecture), including Louis Kahn, Jørn Utzon and Carlo Scarpa, looking at how their buildings celebrate the processes of construction (Frampton 1995). Interestingly, in Frampton's writing there is also a suggestion that these issues have a further political dimension, and I will return to look at this in more detail in Chapter 5 in attempting to define what might constitute an effectively 'critical phenomenology' for architecture. Less well known but not less important is the writing of Marco Frascari, whose early design experience in the office of Carlo Scarpa provided much of the inspiration for his later theoretical work. In an often-reprinted essay he described the links between visual and tactile experience, where tectonic details contribute to a narrative encountered through the embodied experience of movement:

> In architecture, feeling a handrail, walking up steps or between walls, turning a corner and noting the sitting of a beam in a wall, are coordinated elements of visual and tactile sensations. The location of those details gives birth to the conventions that tie a meaning to a perception. The conception

> of the architectural space achieved in this way is the result of the association of the visual images of details, gained through the phenomenon of indirect vision, with the geometrical proposition embodied in forms, dimensions, and location, developed by touching and by walking through buildings.
>
> (Frascari 1984: 506)

In the same essay Frascari also proposed another form of reversibility, this time based on the word 'technology', which he interpreted as a chiasm or intertwining of two related meanings. On the one hand, the *logos* of *techne* meaning, broadly, 'knowledge of construction', relates to the conventional instrumental view of technology as simply a technical means to an end, but on the other hand the *techne* of *logos* also implies the 'construction of knowledge'; the notion that out of a process of making, ideas and concepts can begin to emerge. This combination of meanings echoes our earlier distinction between 'knowing that' and 'knowing how', while suggesting that the former is, in fact, a consequence of the latter. In other words, the growth of conceptual knowledge is based on what Donald Schön famously called 'reflection-in-action'; an ongoing process of critical reflection on the emerging outcomes of practice (Schön 1991: 49–69).

Alongside the more common preoccupation with the materiality and tectonics of construction there is also another form of material narrative that architects should be careful to consider. This is what we might call a 'tectonics of occupation', referring to the way that many buildings contain physical traces of their use accumulated gradually over their lifetime. Rather like Merleau-Ponty's idea of a progressively emerging self – the result of that history we carry forward with us like an ever-rolling snowball – buildings also have a history of their own encounters with the world; one that we often refer to rather dismissively as simply the 'patina of age'. In fact, this is what gives all buildings some degree of individuality, regardless of what is so often the relative anonymity of their original construction. One example is the relentless action of an unpredictable climate which, over time, allows even mass-produced materials to eventually betray their own uniqueness, as a number of architectural writers have also usefully shown (Mostafavi and Leatherbarrow 1993; Hill 2012). Likewise, a building can also respond differently to the actions of its users, transforming itself from a generic container into a unique record of its occupation. The common example of names carved into a school desk, as described by the architect Lars Lerup, suggests that many people feel more comfortable in spaces that invite their appropriation, even if this personalization sometimes involves acts of 'creative destruction' (Lerup 1977: 129f).

## Rather like Merleau-Ponty's idea of a progressively emerging self – the result of that history we carry forward with us like an ever-rolling snowball – buildings also have a history of their own encounters with the world.

Merleau-Ponty was also inspired by this sense of personality that accumulates in 'cultural objects' – a confirmation of the existence of others, as well as, by reflection, ourselves:

> Not only do I have a physical world and live surrounded by soil, air, and water, I have around me roads, plantations, villages, streets, churches, a bell, utensils, a spoon, a pipe. Each of these objects bears as an imprint the mark of the human action it serves. Each one emits an atmosphere of humanity that might be only vaguely determined (when it is a matter of some footprints in the sand), or rather highly determined (if I explore a recently evacuated house from top to bottom).
> 
> (Merleau-Ponty 2012: 363)

When confronted with a historical artefact, he described it as the 'speaking trace of an existence', again being fascinated by the combination of individuality and sociality:

> In the cultural object, I experience the near presence of others under a veil of anonymity. One uses the pipe for smoking, the spoon for eating, or the bell for summoning, and the perception of a cultural world could be verified through the perception of a human act and of another man.
>
> (Merleau-Ponty 2012: 363)

There is, of course, another dimension to this reading of the building as the site of action, alongside the historical narrative implied by the traces of previous uses. This is the idea that the building offers its users 'affordances' for future action, as described in Chapter 2, in relation to the idea of motor cognition. If functions can be signalled by the configuration of building forms then this provides an important means of engaging the bodily actions of building users. As already suggested, there is a potential danger in pursuing a tight fit of form and function, where future uses are too rigidly defined and spaces risk becoming inflexible. There are interesting lessons to be learned from those designers who set out to engage users more directly, encouraging the continual reappropriation of space through creative improvisation. In recent years this can be seen in the work of the Dutch architects Aldo van Eyck and Herman Hertzberger, and currently in a whole range of younger practices working under the banner of 'spatial agency' (Awan et al. 2011).

This kind of openness towards a future of unpredictable possibilities was also suggested by the French philosopher Paul Ricoeur. While usually associated with the more conservative tendencies of historical hermeneutics – the practice of close textual interpretation aimed at recovering 'lost' or hidden meanings in religious writings – Ricoeur has also suggested what amounts to a radical reorientation of hermeneutic efforts in focusing instead on what new meanings a text might, in fact, make possible. In other words, what he describes is a double process of interpretation: of the 'space behind the work' (understanding the intentions of its author) and, even more importantly, the space 'in front of the work', understanding the experience that it makes possible for its future readers, or in our case, building users (Ricoeur 1981: 141).

This idea also illustrates the inherent richness of Merleau-Ponty's layered model of temporality: the idea that what we usually call the 'present moment' is actually a complex layering of recent past and imminent future (Merleau-Ponty 2012: 439f). This is how he described it as expressed in a painting, where a temporal sequence is suggested by the depiction of a process of movement:

> **The painting itself would offer to my eyes almost the same thing offered them by real movements: a series of appropriately mixed, instantaneous glimpses along with, if a living thing is involved, attitudes unstably suspended between a before and an after – in short, the outsides of a change of place which the spectator would read from the imprint it leaves.**
>
> **(Merleau-Ponty 1964a: 184f)**

Another example drawn from my own experience of materiality within a museum building also supports the other claim I have made for a kind of symmetry between two kinds of tectonic expression. Firstly, the tectonics of construction, as expressed in the traces of the process of making, and secondly, what I have called the tectonics of occupation, meaning the accumulating traces of use. The New Art Gallery in Walsall, near Birmingham, designed by Caruso St John Architects, is, in basic terms, a concrete box lined with timber. This timber panelling follows the same layout as the boards used for the concrete shuttering, allowing a direct juxtaposition of the textures of the timber lining and the board-marked concrete. This visual link provides a clear suggestion of the way in which the concrete wall was made, even though it does not literally use the same pieces of timber. Another detail that hints more directly at the role of the body in the construction process appears to be less deliberate and is also much easier to overlook. On the upper landing of the main staircase a number of partial footprints can be seen; fragments of builders' boot marks cast permanently into the concrete floor. While the power-float machines used to finish the concrete would normally smooth these over, in this case, it seems that the builders have not quite managed to successfully 'cover their tracks'. The result provides a subtle record of the bodily movements of the original builders, evidence of a ghostly presence, like the engraved tombstones in the floor of a church. The fact that these permanent traces also appear alongside the more transient footmarks of the building's users invites us in a subtle way to connect how the building was made to the future possibilities of how it might be occupied.

Caruso St John Architects, New Art Gallery, Walsall, 2000.

Caruso St John Architects, New Art Gallery, Walsall.

Caruso St John Architects, New Art Gallery, Walsall; second-floor landing.

A kind of symmetry between two kinds of tectonic expression: firstly, the tectonics of construction, as expressed in the traces of the process of making, and secondly, what I have called the tectonics of occupation, meaning the accumulating traces of use.

### Living materiality and environmental ethics

One sense in which materiality is infused with personality comes from the fact that it has been 'taken up' and put to work in the service of human projects. The relevance of the history that results from this process is what Paul Ricoeur was referring to when he claimed that: 'we understand ourselves only by the long detour of the signs of humanity deposited in cultural works' (Ricoeur 1981: 143). But alongside this somewhat accidental accumulation of the traces of human endeavour, there is also a sense in which technical artefacts are deliberately designed to function as quasi-human proxies. This is the case with many everyday devices that duplicate the actions of human agents, as described, for example, by Bruno Latour in his analysis of a simple overhead door-closer (Latour 1988: 301). Latour took great delight in pointing out what happens when these devices begin to malfunction. In this case, the materiality of the mechanism itself seems to reassert its own form of agency. This is mainly a result of the physical capacities of the material, or what we might better call its particular *propensities*. In other words, the extent to which a material might perform more effectively when used in a particular way. This of course recalls Louis Kahn's idea that there are certain things that a brick 'wants' to be. Wood and slate, for instance, have another kind of propensity based on the distinctive directionality in their cellular structure. They can both be more easily cut and worked along or in parallel to the grain, and this gives them their pronounced visual and physical characteristics.

There is also a reminder here of our earlier discussion regarding the nuances of the French word for 'meaning'. If *sens* can be translated as both *meaning* and *direction*, then perhaps this is a clue towards the 'meaning of a material', whereby a material propensity or agency is the direction in which it wants to go. This idea is also reminiscent of the Chinese concept of *shi*, which can mean both 'position' and 'potential'. It is explained in a useful way by the political theorist Jane Bennett in her book *Vibrant Matter*, which also looks at how complex technical assemblages take on quasi-human qualities:

> *Shi* is the style, energy, propensity, trajectory, or élan inherent to a specific arrangement of things. Originally a word used in military strategy, *shi* emerged in the description of a good general who must be able to read and then ride the *shi* of a configuration of moods, winds, historical trends, and armaments: *shi* names the dynamic force emanating from a spatio-temporal configuration rather than from any particular element within it.
>
> (Bennett 2010: 35)

We could therefore say, in Merleau-Ponty's terms, that our initial grasp of the 'meaning' of a space comes from a sense of its potential for occupation. And likewise, in being solicited to reach out and 'meet it halfway', we are ourselves being drawn in a particular direction. Thus we could say that our grasp of a material affordance is based on a similar sense of its possibilities and limits. What emerges from this is a kind of agency or 'aliveness' within the very fabric of the world, and it is this that Merleau-Ponty had also suggested in his later ontology of the flesh. The reversibility of flesh, as we have already seen, implies that both bodies and objects should be seen as 'living' matter, at least insofar as they have an awareness of each other, in the sense that they can both register the results of their interactions.

## Our grasp of a material affordance is based on a similar sense of its possibilities and limits. What emerges from this is a kind of agency or 'aliveness' within the very fabric of the world.

One source of inspiration for Merleau-Ponty's view is the earlier work of Henri Bergson, although he was keen to distance himself from the more mystical aspects of Bergson's famous concept of vitalism. This was the idea that all living organisms are animated by some kind of mysterious force, or vital energy. His concern to avoid accusations of vitalism is also echoed by a number of contemporary philosophers, particularly those working in the emerging area of what has become known as 'new materialism'. This group of thinkers that might also be broadly characterized as post-humanists is also trying to escape the problems of traditional binary categorization. As we have seen already, Bruno Latour's actor–network theory challenges the division between human and non-human actors, and likewise Donna Haraway's concept of the 'cyborg' blurs the human–machine distinction (Haraway 1991). Alongside this, technological developments are also breaking down traditional categories. For instance, new advances in medicine, such as gene therapy and organ replacement, are forcing us to question our previous understanding of what constitutes a human agent. A number of important writers have been directly influenced by Merleau-Ponty's later philosophy, including Jane Bennett, William Connolly, Katherine Hayles and Diana Coole (Coole and Frost 2010).

Environmental philosophers have also recently contributed to this radical process of rethinking, proposing for example that we consider the earth itself as a single extended living organism. James Lovelock's famous Gaia theory is perhaps the most obvious example of this, suggesting that we think of the world as an interacting network of self-regulating ecosystems (Lovelock 1979). There are obvious ethical consequences to this levelling of the status of human and non-human actors, already suggested by John Dewey's reminder that we should not forget that we are not simply self-sufficient selves. The objects, buildings and landscapes around us are, in fact, part of who we are as human beings, and we should therefore be more careful to look after them, just as we do (usually) with our own bodies:

> **The epidermis is only in the most superficial way an indication of where an organism ends and its environment begins. There are things inside the body that are foreign to it, and there are things outside of it that belong to it ...**

> On the lower scale, air and food materials ... on the higher, tools, whether the pen of the writer or the anvil of the blacksmith, utensils and furnishings, property, friends and institutions – all the supports and sustenances without which a civilised life cannot be. ... The need that is manifest in the urgent impulsions that demand completion through what the environment – and it alone – can supply, is a dynamic acknowledgment of this dependence of the self for wholeness upon its surroundings.
>
> (Dewey 1980/1934: 59)

As we all rely on a constant supply of support from our environment, this might even encourage us to think of a building itself as a living organism, which could likewise be seen as a self-regulating system working in symbiosis with its own environment. In fact, this is an idea put forward by the architect Ken Yeang in his book on *The Green Skyscraper*. Here, the building is described as a series of open-ended systems embedded in its immediate environment, interacting with its surroundings in a constant exchange of energies (Yeang 1999).

As we all rely on a constant supply of support from our environment, this might even encourage us to think of a building itself as a living organism, which could likewise be seen as a self-regulating system working in symbiosis with its own environment.

In Chapter 5 we will return again to Merleau-Ponty's preoccupation with reversibility, but this time in relation to the interplay between experience and forms of expression. However, having seen how contemporary thinkers are 'putting the life back' into materials, it is interesting to see how Merleau-Ponty felt about our more common tendency to take it out. The following quotation describes what can happen, for example, when human artefacts become museum exhibits, even though many would now disagree with this rather dated view of the museum experience. It is, however, a useful reminder of what also happens in the making of philosophical concepts, when lived experience is abstracted into the 'frozen' forms of what Merleau-Ponty called 'objective thought':

> The Museum makes the painters as mysterious for us as octopi or lobsters. It transforms these works created in the fever of a life into marvels from another world, and in its pensive atmosphere and under its protective glass, the breath which sustained them is no more than a feeble flutter on their surface. The Museum kills the vehemence of painting as the library, Sartre said, changes writings that were originally a man's gestures into 'messages'. It is the historicity of death. And there is a historicity of life of which the museum provides no more than a fallen image.
> 
> (Merleau-Ponty 1964b: 63)

CHAPTER 5

# Creativity and innovation

## From *spoken* to *speaking* speech

Despite the common assumption, especially prevalent in architecture, that phenomenology is fundamentally backward-looking, I have been trying to show how Merleau-Ponty offers a radically alternative view. While apparently taking us back to a time before philosophy to show how our ideas are grounded in experience, this should not be taken to mean that he is trying to recover something 'lost' – whether it is lost experiences, lost places or lost meanings. On the contrary, Merleau-Ponty was, in fact, trying to explain how meaning emerges dynamically within the process of our unfolding experience. Both constrained and enabled by our physical and cultural circumstances, we have all, in a sense, had to *learn* how to experience the world. So, there is at least one major thing that architects can draw from this philosophy: a better understanding of the contribution that our built environments can make to this process of learning: 'Our actions and our given surroundings are the starting point of our self-knowledge, each of us being for himself a stranger to which things hold up a mirror' (Merleau-Ponty 1964b: 73).

### Seeing through painting

Merleau-Ponty therefore offers us an alternative vision of phenomenology as a forward-looking method of discovery. This also helps to explain his interest in the process of making art, which he likewise saw as the outcome of a particular form of experience. In his view, the artist makes a painting as a way of seeing the world, or in other words, the artist experiences the world through the *act* of making a painting. Images are therefore not seen as a 'record' of experience; they are the artist's way of having that experience as such. Merleau-Ponty also suggested that, for the viewer, rather than seeing the work as an object, we are instead being invited to 'see according to it', and therefore in some sense to relive the artist's experience in our own bodily response to the image:

> Things have an internal equivalent in me; they arouse in me a carnal formula of their presence. Why shouldn't these [correspondences] in their turn give rise to some [external] visible shape in which anyone else would recognize those motifs which support his own inspection of the world?
>
> (Merleau-Ponty 1964a: 164)

So, whether it is the artist making the work or the viewer who is looking at it, both are seeing the world in a new way through the medium of the work. This goes some way to explain what Merleau-Ponty meant by the 'reversibility' of experience and expression: if to express the world in paintings is an elaborate form of perception, then perhaps all perception should be considered at least a nascent form of expression. Perhaps a better demonstration of this idea comes with art forms that involve the moving body, such as works of contemporary dance that are developed through the process of 'contact improvisation'. This involves one performer moving in response to the movements of another, although it is not always clear at any moment who is following who. In this situation one performer's perception of the other happens through the very act of performing, and therefore out of this perception they are, at the same time, creating a visible form of expression.

## In his view, the artist makes a painting as a way of seeing the world, or, in other words, the artist experiences the world through the *act* of making a painting.

As we saw in Chapter 2, according to the principles of motor cognition, what we perceive in a given situation is only what we are able to respond to. In other words, what 'shows up' for us in an environment is only what we have the bodily skills to enable us to 'cope' with. So, as we have seen already, our initial reaction to the affordance of a space is to invoke the bodily routines that we will need to engage with it. Therefore, if our actions are prefigured in our perceptions, then we could even say that they *are* those very perceptions; that is, we could define perception as the coordination of behaviour between the body and the environment (Maturana and Varela 1992: 231–235). This was also part of Merleau-Ponty's long-standing critique of the traditional empiricist view of perception, in which the body is simply a 'receiving' device passively bombarded with incoming stimulations. His alternative, as we have seen, involved a more proactive process where the body reaches out towards the world, moving in response to its solicitations, and thereby already engaged in a form of behaviour. It is this behavioural aspect of the process of perceiving that Merleau-Ponty described as our first act of expression. In other words – and whether we intend it or not – our behaviour, as manifest in our movement, is also already a form of communication. This is how he described it in one of his key essays on art, 'Indirect Language and the Voices of Silence' (1960):

> **The movement of the artist tracing his arabesque in infinite matter amplifies, but also prolongs, the simple marvel of oriented locomotion or grasping movements. Already in its pointing gestures the body not only flows over into a world whose schema it bears in itself but possesses this world at a distance rather than being possessed by it ... All perception, all action which presupposes it, and in short every human use of the body is already primordial expression.**
>
> **(Merleau-Ponty 1964c: 67)**

So, while the painting may appear to be simply the final outcome of an experience, it should also be seen as the beginning of an ongoing process. This is one consequence of what has been called the 'paradoxical logic of expression', as the philosopher Donald Landes has usefully described it (Landes 2013a). It also implies that becoming an artist involves behaving as an artist does, learning to perceive the world through the act of making art, rather than simply learning how to make paintings. We might also usefully think of an architect as operating in a similar way, perceiving the world through the process of redesigning it. Being an architect, of course, also involves adopting a certain lifestyle that includes a whole assemblage of behaviours, accumulating what Pierre Bourdieu has called social and cultural 'capital'. A key element of the *habitus* of any practising architect is the ability to experience the world by drawing it, and through this process of drawing – which Andy Clark would call 'scaffolded' thinking – to discover new ways of transforming it (Clark 2003: 11).

**Whether we intend it or not, our behaviour, as manifest in our movement, is also already a form of communication.**

### The language of experience

If we experience the world through these particular patterns of behaviour – behaviour which is augmented by tools – then it would seem reasonable to ask what contribution these tools make to the nature of the experience itself. As we have seen already in Chapter 2, the first of these tools is our own biological body, through which we have learnt to experience the world by developing our own particular body schemas. We might also describe these schemas as particular styles of bodily comportment, through which a 'world' becomes available to us, as with Uexküll's concept of the *Umwelt*, which is structured by the body and behaviour of the organism.

We have also seen how Merleau-Ponty explained the intrinsic relation between perception and action, the sense in which bodily movements generate perceptions, just as perceptions solicit further bodily movements. By connecting experience and expression he also went on to suggest that particular styles or habits of movement create particular types of experience. They do this partly by invoking the social and cultural memories embedded in those forms of behaviour. These memories are manifest in the movements of those around us who, in their turn, respond to our ongoing behaviour, all of which is influenced by our shared understanding of the codes and conventions of particular social situations. The best way to explain this is through the example of language, which Merleau-Ponty himself returned to many times in his career. For him it served as a paradigm for the influence of cultural habits on our perceptions, based on the idea that language is best understood as a form of expressive behaviour.

If we recall the evolutionary argument that language began with unconscious bodily gestures, then this link with patterns of behaviour becomes even more explicit (Corballis 2002). The cultural dimension comes from what I would like to call the 'deficit and surplus model' of language, which I hope will also illustrate the creative aspect of communication. This model suggests that when we attempt to communicate in words we end up saying both less and more than we intended, thereby generating both a deficit and a surplus in relation to the thought we were trying to express. The fleeting impression of the passing moment or the 'gut reactions' to unfolding experience can never be captured comprehensively in the ready-made phrases that language, as a pre-existing system, offers up. But the fact that we have to make do with this anonymous language is balanced by an unexpected benefit that arises from the fact that language has been created by others, which gives it a rich collective history. Rather than arriving fully formed, language emerges over time, as a result of people's attempts to make use of it; from previous efforts to capture fleeting thoughts as they continually bubble up and slip away. This means that it also carries more along with it than the present user can ever anticipate, suggesting ideas in the mind of the listener based on their own previous personal experiences. What is sometimes referred to as the baggage that linguistic 'containers' inevitably bring with them suggests additional layers of meaning in the minds of the hearers that go beyond the original intention. This results in a surplus of expression which benefits both the listener and the speaker, because, as Merleau-Ponty pointed out, 'my spoken words surprise me myself and teach me my thought' (Merleau-Ponty 1964c: 88).

When we attempt to communicate in words we end up saying both less and more than we intended, thereby generating both a deficit and a surplus in relation to the thought we were trying to express.

Merleau-Ponty was suggesting something here that goes against our common-sense assumptions about language: the commonly accepted notion that thoughts must exist fully formed in the mind prior to our attempts to communicate them. He showed that, in fact, this is only a small part of the story because language itself is also able to bring thoughts to our minds. In other words, thought is *realized* through the act of speaking, as opposed to being simply represented by it. Thinking, in a sense, 'reaches out' for language in order to express itself more precisely, as he suggested in this passage from his important late essay 'On the Phenomenology of Language':

> The significative intention gives itself a body and knows itself by looking for an equivalent in the system of available significations represented by the language I speak and the whole of the writings and culture I inherit. For that speechless want, the significative intention, it is a matter of realizing a certain arrangement of already signifying instruments or already speaking significations (morphological, syntactical, and lexical instruments, literary genres ... etc.) which arouses in the hearer the presentiment of a new and different signification, and which inversely (in the speaker or the writer) manages to anchor this original signification in the already available ones.
>
> (Merleau-Ponty 1964c: 90)

So, while the richness of the world inevitably exceeds the ability of linguistic expression to capture it, language also serves as a set of tools by which worlds are continually being created. Just as tools and buildings offer affordances for types of behaviour, so language offers affordances for that peculiarly human activity that we call 'rational thinking':

> **Thus, by renouncing a part of his spontaneity, by engaging in the world through stable organs and pre-established circuits, man can acquire the mental and practical space that will free him, in principle, from his milieu and thereby allow him to see it.**
>
> **(Merleau-Ponty 2012: 89)**

What Merleau-Ponty was attempting to describe here is the gap that emerges between language and experience. As can be seen in Graham Harman's discussion of the 'as-structure' of experience, when I attempt to 'grasp' an object and describe it – and thereby to communicate it to someone else – I take the object more or less *as* something I have encountered before. In other words, I effectively caricature it as belonging to a general category of related things. While I may have lost something of the uniqueness of the object in all its particularity and richness, there is also something gained in this process of displacement from the singular to the general. Having named the object or labelled it as a certain type of thing, I can easily describe it to others who share the same linguistic currency. I can also now begin to read into it features that it may not actually possess, simply because I assume it must share them with other objects in the same category. This is of course one of the basic principles by which philosophical argument operates, as we saw previously with the metaphor of the container in relation to logical categories. The sociologist John O'Neill, who was one of Merleau-Ponty's early translators and commentators, suggested that this is one of the problems inherent in both philosophical reflection and science as a whole. For instance, in their efforts to analyse individual events in terms of generalized conceptual categories, both disciplines effectively 'liquidate' the uniqueness of an experience in favour of its repeatable and communicable components (O'Neill 1989: 90). This observation also echoes Merleau-Ponty's claim that the museum 'kills the vehemence of painting', by again subsuming an individual expression into the general canon of art-historical movements.

While the richness of the world inevitably exceeds the ability of linguistic expression to capture it, language also serves as a set of tools by which worlds are continually being created.

Alongside the apparent trade-off between these benefits and problems of language, it was more important for Merleau-Ponty to understand how language itself tries to overcome its own limits. He did this by making a distinction between what he called 'speaking' and 'spoken' speech, first mentioned in *Phenomenology of Perception* but developed in detail in his later essays (Merleau-Ponty 1964c: 44f; 2012: 202f). 'Spoken speech' referred to the conventional language typically used in everyday conversation, including the kind of heavily codified functional terms that we use to communicate factual information. 'Speaking speech', on the other hand, described the more obscure forms of literary language; the kind of poetic expressions that push at the boundaries of convention and test the limits of what can possibly be said. This is often achieved through a deliberate ambiguity in the relation between signifier and signified, as when poets use metaphor and allegory as techniques for opening up multiple possible meanings. It can also happen through the way in which 'spoken speech' is performed by the individual speaker, where a particular acoustic inflection might suggest a whole new layer of meaning:

> The spoken word (the one I utter or the one I hear) is pregnant with a meaning which can be read in the very texture of the linguistic gesture (to the point that a hesitation, an alteration of the voice, or the choice of a certain syntax suffices to modify it), and yet is never contained in that gesture, every expression always appearing to me as a trace ... and every attempt to close our hand on the thought which dwells in the spoken word leaving only a bit of verbal material in our fingers.
>
> (Merleau-Ponty 1964c: 89)

It could be argued that the ambiguity of 'speaking speech' is also what allows language as a system to continue to develop, as it provides a mechanism for the invention of new forms of expression and for the standard lexicon to evolve and expand. To explain this Merleau-Ponty borrowed a phrase from André Malraux, claiming a positive and productive role for the kind of deviations from conventional usage often encountered in expressive language: 'It is just this process of "coherent deformation" of available significations which arranges them in a new sense and takes not only the hearers *but the speaking subject as well* through a decisive *step*' (Merleau-Ponty 1964c: 91).

Hence one might describe what poetry does with words as a kind of 'thickening of the surface' of language, in the sense that – as with a tectonically articulated architecture – it draws attention to its own 'materiality' rather than any obvious semantic reference. This is also a useful reminder of the limitations of the so-called 'language' of postmodernist architecture, which also tended towards banality in its fixation on simplistic figurative references. Instead, by resisting the easy conversion of signs into stereotypical meanings, a more abstract and ambiguous approach to formal expression offers a way to maintain the potential to express new meanings – a benefit which is, of course, also tempered with the risk of being dismissed as meaningless:

> **Because he returns to the source of silent and solitary experience on which culture and the exchange of ideas have been built in order to know it, the artist launches his work just as a man once launched the first word, not knowing whether it will be anything more than a shout, whether it can detach itself from the flow of individual life in which it originates and give the independent existence of an identifiable meaning.**
>
> **(Merleau-Ponty 1964b: 19)**

This suggests that successful communication involves both replication and reinvention, as we saw above when Merleau-Ponty claimed that even new expressions must be anchored in those already available. This also seems to slightly contradict his distinction between speaking and spoken speech, as it thus becomes impossible to draw a definitive boundary between them.

One might describe what poetry does with words as a kind of 'thickening of the surface' of language, in the sense that – as with a tectonically articulated architecture – it draws attention to its own 'materiality'.

### Between spontaneity and repetition

Another way of understanding this emergence of new forms in language is by looking again at behavioural practices such as social conventions and habits. Like language they also have a vital double function, being both tools for discovery and forms of expression. As with the limitations inherent in pre-existing patterns of speech, the bodily routines acquired from previous experiences are never quite fully adequate for each new situation. But there are also two sides to this social equation: however closely we might try to conform to the behavioural norms of a given setting, our actual bodily performances inevitably fall short. In other words, even well-practised habitual actions can never be perfectly reproduced owing to the inherent inertia and unpredictability of our own physical embodiment. As suggested by Merleau-Ponty in his analysis of expressive speech, this 'thickness' or ambiguity in the material embodiment of behaviour again appears to support the critical agency of the individual. According to Gail Weiss's recent analysis of Merleau-Ponty's understanding of habit, 'even in the most sedimented patterns of conduct, ambiguity and indeterminacy are nonetheless present, guaranteeing that the repetition of old habits will never be a complete repetition of the same' (Weiss 2008b: 96).

This observation highlights the important gap between intention and realization involved in any individual action; that inevitable element of slippage between the behaviour that seems to be called for and that which is actually performed. It is this gap at the very centre of the process of what we might call 'social reproduction' (the process by which cultural habits are passed on and, at the same time, inevitably modified) that seems to be something of a blind spot in the later account of the *habitus* given by Pierre Bourdieu (Bourdieu 1977; 1990). For Merleau-Ponty it is our own embodiment that offers the promise of creative adaptation and change, as Gail Weiss again usefully pointed out: 'Rather than presenting transformation and sedimentation as mutually exclusive binaries of openness and closure where each presents a threat to the other, Merleau-Ponty locates innovation at the very heart of sedimentation, and his primary example of how this occurs is through language' (Weiss 2008b: 96). In other words, the very inadequacy of our attempts to reproduce habitual behaviours is precisely what allows space for new patterns to emerge. As variations in behaviour solicit new responses from those around us – and the most effective ones begin to be repeated and thus preserved as they are passed on – the canon of available actions gradually increases and evolves. Thus, by attempting to take up and reproduce existing conventions and while doing it, inevitably, always less than perfectly, we are – rather like overzealous actors – effectively rewriting the scripts we were attempting to perform.

Merleau-Ponty's account of the acquisition and execution of behavioural routines therefore suggests a somewhat counterintuitive conclusion: innovation is not only possible within these processes; it is, thanks to our embodiment, actually inevitable. This insight is vital to understanding the creativity and criticality inherent in all embodied activity – whether we are, like Merleau-Ponty, looking at art, literature, philosophy or even architecture. The key thing is that all these activities involve a certain level of creative randomness in the sense that mistakes are inevitably generated, even by genuine attempts at repetition. These 'copying errors' or mutations in the 'DNA' of behaviour will generate new significations that can be retained if they turn out to be useful. In other words, there is a version of 'Darwinian selection' among cultural forms that preserves beneficial mutations, such as when popular neologisms like 'texting' and 'trolling' are added to the official lexicon of the language.

## Innovation is not only possible within these processes; it is, thanks to our embodiment, actually inevitable.

## Reverting to type

From an architectural point of view this principle has a number of important corollaries, particularly within the process of design. We can think, for example, of the way that new forms are generated as an interplay between spontaneity and repetition. This is especially so in the early stages of design, where we are still unsure precisely *what* it is that we are designing. One way of understanding this stage of the process is to think in terms of building 'types', which might be either consciously or unconsciously applied. These may be historical models or precedents for specific functional forms, or they may be drawn from our own personal 'archive' of previous design solutions. The use of historic types as a source for design ideas was first formalized in the late eighteenth century, initially in the writings of the French architect Quatremère de Quincy (Lavin 1992). He also made an important distinction between the 'type' and the 'model', in terms of the degree of flexibility allowed for the individual designer in reinterpreting the historic precedent. Using models as a design method was, in principle, to be avoided because it involved trying to replicate historic forms in precise detail. Types, on the other hand, contained only the underlying rules or principles on which the previous models might have been based. These rules were sufficiently loose and generic to allow the historic type to be adapted to suit new circumstances. By following the principle of 'coherent deformation' of the previously established 'significations', the new form would maintain some level of historical continuity, while also satisfying its new functional or contextual requirements.

As a design method, typology underwent a revival in the 1960s as part of the post-war critique and reassessment of modernism, and this was also inspired partly by the growing impact of phenomenology in architecture. This was especially dramatic in the work of those postmodernist architects who advocated a revival of historical styles, although some of the most important work was done in the area of urban theory by writers such as Aldo Rossi and Colin Rowe (Rowe and Koetter 1978; Rossi 1982). They both promoted the idea of the city as a collage of fragments, with old buildings adapted to new uses, and in Rossi's case, this extended to the new buildings he designed as reinterpretations of historical types. This approach was also at the heart of what was later called Critical Regionalism, where the historical types being critically reinterpreted were based more specifically on local or regional sources (Frampton 1983; Lefaivre and Tzonis 2003). In Frampton's version the notion of type was expanded to include local materials and craft traditions, based partly on the nineteenth-century writings of the German architect Gottfried Semper, on what he called, in 1851, *The Four Elements of Architecture* (Semper 1989). In Semper's case the elements were neither formal nor functional types, but rather tectonic processes; the four crafts that he felt were the ultimate origin of architecture: masonry, ceramics, joinery and weaving.

I will return to consider Frampton's views on the 'politics of the tectonic' towards the end of this chapter, but for now it is worth mentioning one other example of 'coherent deformation' that also has a tectonic dimension. This is the creative practice known as *bricolage* that involves the reappropriation of old forms for new uses. This can sometimes involve the salvaging of historic architectural fragments when redundant buildings are demolished and the most valuable elements are reused elsewhere. A good example was the medieval practice of reusing *spolia* rescued from the ruins of Roman temples (Hansen 2003). In recent times, *bricolage* has re-emerged as a reaction to the general scarcity of resources, as a way of avoiding the more costly process of producing purpose-made building components. *Bricolage* in architecture therefore involves the use of cheaper off-the-shelf components, often designed for a specific purpose, but also able to be put to use for something else. It was Merleau-Ponty's great friend Claude Lévi-Strauss who famously turned this practice into a metaphor, using it to explain how myths are created out of the agglomeration of earlier narratives (Lévi-Strauss 1966). Interesting architectural examples include the work of the American practice Mockbee Coker, as well as younger designers such as Teddy Cruz and others featured in the 'Spatial Agency' database (Ryker 1995; Awan et al. 2011).

## Material methods

As we have seen, Merleau-Ponty was particularly interested in the way that new language can be created. He saw this as one consequence of the materiality of the medium itself, and this led him to a position familiar to many structuralist and post-structuralist thinkers. In this passage, which contains a hint about the importance of the relations between linguistic signs, he used the term 'empirical language' to refer to what he later called 'spoken' speech:

> **But what if language expresses as much by what is between words as by the words themselves? By that which it does not 'say' as by what it 'says'? And what if, hidden in empirical language, there is a second order language in which signs once again lead the vague life of colors, and in which significations never free themselves completely from the intercourse of signs?**
> 
> **(Merleau-Ponty 1964c: 45)**

It was from Ferdinand de Saussure (1857–1913) that he took on the idea that language operates as a 'system of differences', where meaning depends as much on the relationships between linguistic signs as it does on their relations to objects. While some later thinkers went on to deny that language has any meaningful relation to reality – as implied by Jacques Derrida's notorious claim that there is 'nothing outside the text' – Merleau-Ponty instead wanted to maintain this connection, at least as a goal towards which language aspires. He saw this attempt to reach out to grasp the world as inherent to the very 'project' of language, while accepting that it will never fully 'exhaust' what it attempts to describe. As there is no such thing as a perfect language, then meaning is always left open to uncertainty; held in abeyance, one might say, through what Derrida called a continuous process of 'deferral'. But this still leaves a dilemma as to the nature of these inherent limits, which Merleau-Ponty suggested by asking this useful, but somewhat mischievous, question: 'Why, then, do we not methodically produce perfect images of the world, arriving at a universal art purged of all personal art, just as the universal language would free us of all the confused relationships that lurk in existent languages?' (Merleau-Ponty 1964a: 172).

It was from Ferdinand de Saussure that he took on the idea that language operates as a 'system of differences', where meaning depends as much on the relationships between linguistic signs as it does on their relations to objects.

So, it is not that language could ever give us the 'true' meaning of things, but rather that it gives us a way in which the world can become meaningful *for us*. Like perception, when we understand it as a means of reaching out and engaging with the world, language offers us a medium for both experiencing and expressing it. The gaps and 'confused relationships' that lurk within any language are therefore the very things that allow room for meaning itself to emerge, reminding us that all language is based, in principle, on metaphor:

> It goes without saying that language is oblique and autonomous, and that its ability to signify a thought or a thing directly is only a secondary power derived from the inner life of language. Like the weaver, the writer works on the wrong side of his material. He has to do only with language, and it is thus that he suddenly finds himself surrounded by meaning.
>
> (Merleau-Ponty 1964c: 44f)

Merleau-Ponty also looked at painting to help him understand this process of emergence; a process he previously called the 'springing forth of reason in a world that it did not create' (Merleau-Ponty 2012: 57). Towards the end of *Phenomenology of Perception* he introduced this connection of language and painting, highlighting the distinction between the two forms of speech that we saw him develop in his later essays:

> For the painter or the speaking subject, the painting and the speech are not the illustration of an already completed thought, but rather the appropriation of this very thought. This is why we have been led to

> distinguish between a secondary speech, which conveys an already acquired thought and an originary speech which first brings this thought into existence for us just as it does for others.
>
> (Merleau-Ponty 2012: 409)

On this model both painting and writing could be seen as creative tools of discovery (Merleau-Ponty 1970: 13), rather like a fishing net dipped into the 'stream of consciousness' to catch a fleeting half-formed thought before it slips away. Scholars of language evolution have also likened this process to the growth of a mangrove forest in a swamp, which produces relatively stable land masses by gradually trapping debris within the tangles of its root system (Clark 2003: 80–82). If words likewise offer 'islands' of stability on which more complex thought constructions can be built, then this might also help to explain how drawing and sketching can also support an artist's thinking process.

One of Merleau-Ponty's examples came from the work of Henri Matisse, based on a film of the artist in action which revealed the process of 'thinking through drawing':

> A camera once recorded the work of Matisse in slow motion. The impression was prodigious … That same brush which, seen with the naked eye, leaped from one act to another, was seen to meditate in a solemn and expanding time … to try ten possible movements, dance in front of the canvas, brush it lightly several times, and crash down finally like a lightning stroke upon the one line necessary.
>
> (Merleau-Ponty 1964c: 45)

Matisse's apparent hesitation in front of the drawing involved a choice of which line to commit to, which at the same time meant deciding which of the alternatives to reject. The fact that they all remained visible in the final drawing allowed both the artist and the eventual viewer to retrace the path of the process; again, an echo of the evolutionary mechanism that selects mutations which turn out to be beneficial. This is one reason why exhibitions of architects' sketchbooks can sometimes be more compelling than the actual buildings themselves: seeing these various 'roads not taken' along the journey of design development can often give a better insight into the nature of the creative process. One benefit of the hand-drawn sketch over that of the hard-line CAD image is precisely this ability to retain the traces of previously abandoned lines. This allows the designer to compare a number of alternatives while perhaps working on different areas of a drawing, literally providing a space to think 'between the lines' before deciding which options to commit to and develop further.

This also highlights a dilemma about the early stages of the design process when it is often difficult for the designer to know where to begin. Many student projects, for example, start with an observational exercise involving making drawings of the existing conditions of a place. By drawing the site – as opposed to just photographing it – a series of initial judgements can begin to be made. In deciding what aspects might be most useful to record, other details for the time being can be ignored. It is here where the productive gaps between image and reality begin to create space for the designer's imagination to inhabit. So, the action of drawing the 'world as it is' seems to open it up for change; in other words, to 'loosen the joints' of reality and to allow for things to be reconfigured. Or to use a familiar software analogy, the drawing allows the world to be 'unlocked for editing'.

## The action of drawing the 'world as it is' seems to open it up for change; in other words, to 'loosen the joints' of reality and to allow for things to be reconfigured.

Having opened up a space of possibilities within the drawing, there is then the question of how we progress to the next stage: how do we begin drawing out a new idea that is only half-formed in the imagination? On one level, it seems as if we are driven to try and visualize an emerging idea simply in order to find out what it might look like. Something then happens within the act of drawing that, as Merleau-Ponty says, takes us through a 'decisive step'. Often without realizing it, these first tentative drawings are based on our own personal vocabulary: a repertoire of available graphic significations that allows us to categorize a new idea in terms of something familiar. In other words, we seem to be – at least momentarily – classifying a still vague notion, taking it 'as something' similar to what we have drawn before in order to be able to begin exploring its possibilities. Then, once drawn, we can stand back and inspect it, and allow the image to 'teach us our thought', as Merleau-Ponty said of language. Perhaps we see a way to 'coherently deform' it and make it more like or less like the previous 'model'. This process goes some way to explain the enduring popularity of books that contain catalogues of historic architectural precedents. I am thinking especially of those that are organized by formal and spatial types such as Francis Ching's *Architecture: Form, Space and Order* (Ching 1996).

In architecture the process of drawing allows us to reimagine the world in a more radical way than would be possible without it. One could argue that this is one of the benefits to have resulted from the historical changes in the professional role of the architect. By separating design from the hands-on process of building, the drawing takes on an elevated status. As well as being symbolic of the unique function of the architect it also allows new possibilities for innovative design. Imagine trying to create a building without the aid of drawings and you have a situation similar to that of the pre-modern tradition of vernacular architecture. In that case, the designer and the builder were normally the same person, and the design was usually based more or less directly on a previous building. This would account for the consistency of many historic settlements, where similar building forms were repeated, often over many hundreds of years. When the previously built 'prototypes' were augmented only by the builder's 'working memory', then it was usually only possible to include minor design changes, and then often only at the level of construction details, thanks to the skilled improvisation of the individual craftsman. By contrast, the architectural drawing offers a safe way of simulating and testing new solutions, providing a realm of innovation and experiment without the expense of working at full size.

One of the important ways in which innovation occurs in the process of drawing is through the often unanticipated effects of the chosen technique. This again is where materiality can surprise the designer, just as Merleau-Ponty was surprised by his words. If one thinks of a drawing like a scientific apparatus, set up to test a hypothesis, what comes out at the end is often very useful, even if it is not what the investigator intended. Bruno Latour has recently called this the 'surprise of action', and used an architectural analogy in order to explain it, describing how, even if the scientist appears to construct 'facts', they are never in complete control of their medium:

> **The scientist makes the fact, but whenever we make something we are not in command, we are slightly overtaken by the action: every builder knows that. Thus the paradox of constructivism is that it uses a vocabulary of mastery that no architect, mason, city planner, or carpenter would ever use ... I never act; I am always slightly surprised by what I do. That which acts through me is also surprised by what I do, by the chance to mutate, to change, to bifurcate, the chance that I and the circumstances surrounding me offer to that which has been invited.**
>
> **(Latour 1999: 281)**

What appears within the drawing as the 'surprise' of the designer's action is often also a consequence of the equipment involved. The architectural theorist Marco Frascari, for example, wrote in great detail about the role of traditional drawing instruments. He likened the process of drawing with a pair of compasses to the religious practice of divination, as a means for the designer to create some kind of connection between the realms of the actual and the possible (Frascari 2011: 33, 117–127). In another essay Frascari also described the effects of different kinds of paper used at different stages of the design process, including a student exercise where the whole project was designed and presented on a single panel of white-painted wood (Frascari et al. 2007: 23–33). A good recent example of the influence of the drawing technique on the outcome of the design appears in Peter Zumthor's sketches of the thermal baths at Vals. By using the side of a stick of pastel to create what he later called 'block drawings', the key idea for the atmosphere of the interior space began to emerge. The 'slabs' of colour in these early sketches became a bold composition of free-standing stone masses, with daylight filtering down to illuminate the voids between them (Mindrup 2015: 61–64).

Other design strategies have their own forms of materiality, like Peter Eisenman's use of basic geometrical types as starting points for exploration. By subjecting simple 'Platonic' forms to a process of step-by-step transformation, even these generic shapes can produce unexpected effects. This same combination of constraints and opportunities is also evident within the digital realm, where the particular affordances offered by different software packages can also have a dramatic effect on the outcome. Buildings modelled in Rhino as opposed to SketchUp are often very easy to distinguish, given the two applications' very different abilities to manipulate complex double-curved surfaces.

## This same combination of constraints and opportunities is also evident within the digital realm, where the particular affordances offered by different software packages can also have a dramatic effect on the outcome.

What each of these cases highlights is the important potential for embodied material processes to help generate novel solutions. They can do this in part by escaping the constraints of imposed, top-down intellectual frameworks. Rather than adopting ready-made solutions or preconceived models, many architects work from the 'bottom up', by following what the anthropologist Tim Ingold calls the 'lines of flight' suggested by their chosen materials (Ingold 2013: 102). Whether these materials are physical (i.e. constructional), typological, geometrical or even conceptual, the idea is that all these different 'media' of expression offer their own particular propensities. By pushing against their various resistances new 'possibilities of occupiable form' can be generated

(Eisenman et al. 1987: 169). This can happen in the modelling workshop, as with architects like Frank Gehry, who work directly on physical maquettes, or with self-builders and *bricoleurs* improvising on site with recycled or repurposed components. This last point should also remind us of the creativity inherent in the embodied knowledge of the highly skilled builder; something that is increasingly excluded by the contractual relationships that enforce an absolute split between design and construction. It was traditionally quite common for the architect's construction information to convey only the basic outlines of the design, and for the contractor to 'fill in the gaps' from their own experiential knowledge. Builders would contribute creatively to the project by drawing on their personal experience of contextual factors, such as climate, ground conditions and locally available materials.

In Chapter 4 I described an example of this kind of bodily contribution, as evidenced in the way the building's surfaces carry traces of the construction process. I also suggested that this might be a key characteristic of spaces that invite the occupation of the user, with the result that they become animated with a sense of personality and particularity. These accumulating records of life within the building can also go some way towards subverting its dominant 'meaning'; i.e. questioning the official generic designation of the building as, for example, 'museum', 'school' or 'office'. This idea also echoes Roland Barthes' famous concept of the *punctum,* which he developed in his analysis of photographic images first published in 1980. This idea describes the power of the personal detail which is often overlooked or partially concealed within a photograph, but still retains the power to disrupt the manifest content or accepted meaning of the overall image (Barthes 2000: 25–27).

## Reuse and reinterpretation

Another area in which Merleau-Ponty's ideas on the materiality of language are relevant to architecture is in understanding the enduring appeal of historic buildings which have been adapted to fulfil new functions. I am thinking especially of the recent tendency to convert industrial buildings into art museums, as well as the preference among many contemporary artists for displaying their work in so-called 'found spaces'. One reason for this could be the presence of visual disjunctions that typically occur in 'adaptive reuse', where the original relationship of form and function has often been radically displaced. When the traces of former uses are still evident alongside the new insertions this seems to produce a space with a heightened potential for creative appropriation. There is also the more literal kind of opening up that is often associated with the 'pleasure of ruins', when walls or floors are removed and new views are created between spaces that were previously isolated. This has been usefully described by Fred Scott, in his book *On Altering Architecture*, in terms of the excitement and sense of transgression that often results from these interventions in redundant buildings:

> **For the occupants, the new circulation of the altered interior may be like a journey through ruins, taking previously impossible routes, and having new, almost aberrant viewpoints as a result. An altered building explains itself; it is in this way an inhabited ruin … The altered condition may have qualities of exposure that previously one thought of as confined to drawings, such as sectional perspectives.**
>
> (Scott 2008: 171)

This reference to the power of drawing itself as a tool for exploration and discovery suggests a link back to what Merleau-Ponty identified in the slow-motion film of Matisse: a space of hesitation between the lines on the paper that offered the potential for new significations and meanings to emerge.

The preference among many contemporary artists for displaying their work in so-called 'found spaces'. One reason for this could be the presence of visual disjunctions that typically occur in 'adaptive reuse'.

A similar interpretation has been made of work by the video artist Bill Viola, in a book by the performance theorist Carrie Noland that also draws on Merleau-Ponty's work on perception (Noland 2009: 66–72). In the time-lapse video work from 2000, entitled *The Quintet of the Astonished,* five actors' faces are shown performing the five classic emotional expressions of fear, anger, pain, sorrow and joy. By shooting the video at up to 384 frames per second instead of the typical 24, one minute of live action is extended to create 16 minutes of viewing time. The effect is to allow previously unnoticeable movements to suddenly become highly visible, blurring the normal distinctions between one emotional expression and another. This opens up for the viewer's inspection the previously unseen transitions between them, offering a range of still ambiguous new expressions to become available to be assigned to new meanings.

One lesson to be taken from this, as with all the examples discussed, is that the embodied physicality of materials is precisely what puts them beyond our complete control, and at the same time it guarantees that we will be continually surprised by what they produce. Likewise, it is our own bodily materiality that helps us resist the imposition of political power, contrary to what many critics have concluded from reading the later work of Foucault and Bourdieu. And it is a similar point made by Kenneth Frampton in his important work on Critical Regionalism, where he emphasizes the role of materiality and bodily experience in the process of political resistance:

> Two independent channels of resistance proffer themselves against the ubiquity of the Megalopolis and the exclusivity of sight. They presuppose a mediation of the mind/body split in Western thought. They may be regarded as archaic agents with which to counter the potential universality of rootless civilization. The first of these is the tactile resilience of the place-form; the second is the sensorium of the body. These two are posited here as interdependent, because each is contingent on the other. The place-form is inaccessible to sight alone just as simulacra [images or virtual 'simulations'] exclude the tactile capacity of the body.
>
> (Frampton 1988)

Against the oversimplification of Critical Regionalism that has been a tendency in recent years, it might also be argued that traditional regional architectures are themselves inherently critical, in the sense that new ideas are an inevitable outcome of bottom-up processes of material exploration. I am thinking here of the way in which vernacular traditions tend to be based on so-called 'experiential learning', where both design and construction practices are passed on through behavioural routines (Lave and Wenger 1991: 34–37). This direct 'body-to-body' process of learning contrasts with the conceptual model prevalent today, where architectural knowledge is normally communicated through textbooks in a formalized academic setting. This freezing of knowledge in conceptual form tends to act as a brake on innovation, binding practices to fixed principles that are often unable to adapt to changing requirements. By contrast, where you have techniques passed on directly through some form of material embodiment, the inherent looseness and ambiguity of this process can act as a kind of 'engine' of invention. I would argue that this kind of innovation is also more responsive to evolving social needs, as well as being difficult to legislate against from above by the imposition of written rules and regulations.

## It is our own bodily materiality that helps us resist the imposition of political power, contrary to what many critics have concluded from the later work of Foucault and Bourdieu.

Frampton has described this elsewhere as an effort to maintain the value of local distinctiveness and particularity, when so much of global culture seems to be moving towards homogenization. He did this by celebrating three connections that all buildings should try to maintain – the *tactile*, *tectonic* and *telluric* – and which all depend on this idea of uniqueness (Frampton 1983; Jameson 1994: 189–205). The *telluric* involves a connection between the building and the 'materiality' of the site, which may involve both its physical and its historical character. The *tectonic* should capture something of the history of the building's construction, while the *tactile* should both encourage and incorporate the active bodily engagement of the user.

Merleau-Ponty likewise saw embodiment as a means to resist the generalizing effect of 'high-altitude' reflection: the tendency of philosophical thought to 'bask in its acquisitions' and thereby relinquish its connections with experience (Merleau-Ponty 2012: 409). As he said, it is the nature of 'expressive language' to be constantly renewing itself – or at least always striving to renew its inherently unstable grasp on the world:

> Each act of philosophical or literary expression contributes to fulfilling the vow to retrieve the world taken with the first appearance of a language, that is, with the first appearance of a finite system of signs ... Each act of expression realizes for its own part a portion of this project, and by opening a new field of truths, further extends the contract which has just expired. This is possible only through the same 'intentional transgression' which gives us others; and like it the phenomenon of truth, which is theoretically impossible, is known only through the praxis which creates it.
> (Merleau-Ponty 1964c: 95f)

CHAPTER 6

# 'There is nothing outside embodiment'

I hope to have shown in the course of this book that there are many ways in which Merleau-Ponty's ideas can be useful to architects. Having focused on some of the most basic implications of embodiment – in other words, the fact that we are, as human beings, inescapably embodied entities – it should now be clear why Merleau-Ponty's philosophy has so much to offer. To begin with, his concept of the 'flesh' suggests that human bodies share fundamental characteristics with the rest of the material world – all of those living, and apparently non-living, things that provide the 'supports and sustenances' that, as John Dewey reminded us, we rely on to survive. We should therefore reflect on the fundamental interdependence between human life and the surrounding environment, and remember our ultimate responsibility to preserve it for the future. The ethical aspects of our encounters with the material conditions of the world are also apparent in Merleau-Ponty's notion of 'reversibility'; the idea that we can only perceive the world because we are (as bodily beings) also perceivable ourselves. This 'bit of the world' that we call our body is of course also a material entity, and the fact that we can 'perceive with it' also reminds us that all material entities, in a sense, 'perceive us'. In other words, all the things – people and objects – with which we interact in our day-to-day activities, are, however minimally, transformed by this encounter. This process also extends to places, to the extent that they too can register interactions with their users, whose traces of occupation and appropriation provide evidence of the passing of time.

Another aspect of reversibility in Merleau-Ponty's philosophy is the notion of a reciprocal relationship between experience and expression. The idea that experience itself is inherently expressive is based on the fact that perception is a process that involves the whole body. Just as we are able to move around in the world only because we have the ability to perceive it, likewise we can perceive it effectively only because we can move around in it. In other words, our sense of three-dimensional space is grounded in our own three-dimensional embodiment. Beyond this, our feelings about the world are also inevitably betrayed in our bodily comportment, in the sense that the manner in which we move ourselves is already expressive of our gradually emerging beliefs and attitudes. Of the many ways of 'being an architect' one of the most characteristic is the habit of sketching, although this is just one example of a form of behaviour that is both experiential and expressive. As well as being a way of collecting ideas from observation that becomes part of a personal design vocabulary, the act of capturing in simplified form is already the beginning of the process of invention. We can thereby learn to 'see like an architect' through these very particular 'habits of looking', seeing the world *through* the act of drawing, just as Merleau-Ponty described with Cézanne and Matisse.

Another important aspect of the reciprocal connection between the materiality of the body and that of the world is the kind of tectonic sensibility that architects often develop, from their experience of the construction process. While this is not an essential element of every architectural student's education, many schools of architecture place a high priority on the hands-on experience of building. Developing empathy for the capacities of materials and an intuitive grasp of their possibilities and limits are also important transferable skills that apply to many areas of an architect's activity. They can also help in understanding the potential offered by the particular characteristics of a building site, or even how to work within the social context of a complex client organization.

Empathy is also involved in developing a sensibility towards what Merleau-Ponty called the physiognomy of things; that gestural language of form based on our own bodies that gives all objects an emotional dimension. Even more fundamental than this representational aspect of what is sometimes referred to as the 'body image' is the functional role of the 'body schema' that Merleau-Ponty explored in much detail. The idea that we learn to perceive the world through an accumulating repertoire of bodily skills suggests that perception works partly on the basis of prediction of what we expect to happen. It is this that should make designers more careful in arranging spaces for particular functions, aiming for that difficult balance of boredom and novelty that enables people to 'cope with' – and still be surprised by – their everyday environments.

To conclude, it is worth reiterating that Merleau-Ponty is not trying to take us back into a mythical past in which bodies and materials were miraculously conjoined, or when some kind of ideal harmony existed between dwelling and building. Rather, he is simply reminding us that while embodiment is inherent in life, we too often overlook the material dimensions of the things we encounter in our everyday experience – whether these are buildings and objects, or even other people, their words and their patterns of behaviour. If there is a downside to the freedom promised by life in the digital realm, it is this same tendency to succumb to the rhetoric of apparent immateriality and to forget that our only way to access the virtual world is precisely through our bodily interfaces (Hayles 1999).

Even more easily do we forget the materiality of ideas, which, like all objects, have their own inherent limits and possibilities. Thomas Kuhn's 'scientific paradigms' provide a good case in point, showing how conceptual structures actively shape our notions of truth (Kuhn 1970). It is this sensibility towards the inherent resistance of material things – the fact that all things, even concepts, have their 'grain', their patterns and their propensities – that should be the enduring legacy of Merleau-Ponty's overarching philosophy of embodiment. So, rather than simply encouraging us to fetishize expensive materials and elaborately articulated details, Merleau-Ponty instead invites us to consider the inherent materiality of all our tools and techniques, and how this materiality serves to protect us from the arbitrary impositions of top-down control.

This sensibility towards the inherent resistance of material things – the fact that all things, even concepts, have their 'grain', their patterns and their propensities – should be the enduring legacy of Merleau-Ponty's overarching philosophy of embodiment.

The other significant lesson of Merleau-Ponty's philosophical approach is his effective bringing together of phenomenology and structuralism. He also tried to establish an alternative to the dualistic division of subject and object by exploring the fundamental interdependence between these two phenomena. By seeing these two terms as equally abstract and post-rationalized constructions, he offered a way to understand embodied experience as our enduring 'primordial condition'. The vital contribution that our environment makes – in both its physical and cultural structures – should make his work an essential starting point for anyone thinking deeply about architecture.

> Thus along with the world – as the cradle of all significations, as the sense of all senses, and as the ground of all thoughts – we also discovered the means of overcoming the alternatives of realism and idealism, between contingency and absolute reason, and between non-sense and sense. The world, such as we have attempted to reveal it ... is no longer the visible unfolding of a constituting thought, nor a fortuitous collection of parts, and certainly not the operation of a directing thought upon an indifferent matter; rather, the world is the homeland of all rationality.
>
> (Merleau-Ponty 2012: 454)

# Further reading

In recent years a surprising number of introductions to Merleau-Ponty's philosophy have been published, suggesting a strong resurgence of interest across a range of different fields. To my mind, still the most useful – thanks to its clarity and accessibility – is Eric Matthews' book *The Philosophy of Merleau-Ponty* (2002). As an alternative, Taylor Carman's *Merleau-Ponty* (2008) offers a slightly more substantial treatment, and also does an excellent job of pulling together many of the apparently more disparate strands of Merleau-Ponty's work. An earlier book, which presents all his major writings within a useful overarching narrative, is Gary Brent Madison's *The Phenomenology of Merleau-Ponty: A Search for the Limits of Consciousness* (1981). While this book is by no means an easy read, it does provide a convincing explanation of the difficulties inherent in Merleau-Ponty's attempt to test the limits of philosophy itself.

Of course, there is no real substitute for reading Merleau-Ponty's own work, and I sincerely hope this book will have helped encourage more architects to do this. A good place to begin is with the transcripts of the radio broadcasts published as *The World of Perception* (2008), which are relatively jargon-free, having been written for a general audience. Merleau-Ponty's major work is of course *Phenomenology of Perception,* and the new translation by Donald Landes (2012) has made the text far more accessible than the previous version (1962). As 'travelling companions' for what can still sometimes seem like a lonely and difficult journey, I would also recommend one of the two excellent guidebooks that focus specifically on this key text: Monika Langer's book *Merleau-Ponty's Phenomenology of Perception: A Guide and Commentary* (1989) and my former colleague Komarine Romdenh-Romluc's *Merleau-Ponty and Phenomenology of Perception* (2011), which makes good use of explanatory examples and is refreshingly clear in style. And finally, for short explanations of key ideas and definitions of philosophical terms, both *Merleau-Ponty: Key Concepts* (Diprose and Reynolds 2008) and *The Merleau-Ponty Dictionary* (Landes 2013b) are extremely useful to keep within arm's reach.

Within architecture – despite frequent passing references – there are, sadly, few cases of sustained engagement with Merleau-Ponty's work. *On Architecture* by Fred Rush (2009) is a notable exception, although it also happens to have been written by a philosopher. Examples by architects include Dalibor Vesely (2004) and Juhani Pallasmaa (2005; 2009). *The Eyes of the Skin* addresses the important theme of bodily experience in architecture, although – at less than 80 pages – it is probably more useful to think of it as an annotated bibliography. In a similar vein I would also recommend *Questions of Perception: Phenomenology of Architecture* (Holl, Pallasmaa and Pérez-Gómez 2006), which considers the implications of Merleau-Ponty's ideas across both architectural history and design contexts.

# Bibliography

Abel, C. (2015) *The Extended Self: Architecture, Memes and Minds,* Manchester: Manchester University Press.

Abram, D. (1996) *The Spell of the Sensuous: Perception and Language in a More-Than-Human World,* New York: Pantheon.

Alaimo, S. (2010) *Bodily Natures: Science, Environment, and the Material Self,* Bloomington, IN: Indiana University Press.

Andersen, M. A. and Oxvig, H. (eds) (2009) *Paradoxes of Appearing: Essays on Art, Architecture and Philosophy,* Baden, Switzerland: Lars Müller.

Arbib, M. A. and Hesse, M. B. (1986) *The Construction of Reality,* Cambridge: Cambridge University Press.

Archer, M. S. (2000) *Being Human: The Problem of Agency,* Cambridge: Cambridge University Press.

Armstrong, D. F. and Wilcox, S. (2007) *The Gestural Origin of Language,* New York and Oxford: Oxford University Press.

Arnheim, R. (1977) *The Dynamics of Architectural Form: Based on the 1975 Mary Duke Biddle Lectures at the Cooper Union,* Berkeley, CA and London: University of California Press.

Artaud, A. (1958) *The Theater and Its Double,* trans. Richards, M.C. New York: Grove Press.

Awan, N., Schneider, T. and Till, J. (eds) (2011) *Spatial Agency: Other Ways of Doing Architecture*, London: Routledge.

Barad, K. M. (2007) *Meeting the Universe Halfway: Quantum Physics and the Entanglement of Matter and Meaning,* Durham, NC: Duke University Press.

Barbaras, R. (2004) *The Being of the Phenomenon: Merleau-Ponty's Ontology,* trans. Toadvine, T. & Lawlor, L. Bloomington, IN: Indiana University Press.

Barbaras, R. (2006) *Desire and Distance: Introduction to a Phenomenology of Perception,* trans. Milan, P.B. Stanford, CA: Stanford University Press.

Barthes, R. (2000) *Camera Lucida: Reflections on Photography,* trans. Howard, R. London: Vintage.

Beaune, S. A. d. and Coolidge, F. L. (eds) (2009) *Cognitive Archaeology and Human Evolution*, Cambridge: Cambridge University Press.

Bennett, J. (2010) *Vibrant Matter: A Political Ecology of Things,* Durham, NC: Duke University Press.

Bergson, H. (1988) *Matter and Memory* (originally published 1896), trans. Paul, N.M. & Palmer, W.S. New York: Zone Books.

Bermudez, J. L. (2003) *Thinking Without Words,* New York and Oxford: Oxford University Press, 2007.

Bermudez, J. L., Marcel, A. J. and Eilan, N. (eds) (1995) *The Body and the Self*, Cambridge, MA and London: MIT Press.

Berthoz, A. (2000) *The Brain's Sense of Movement,* trans. Weiss, G. Cambridge, MA and London: Harvard University Press.

Bhatt, R. (ed.) (2013) *Rethinking Aesthetics: The Role of Body in Design*, New York: Routledge.

Blackman, L. (2008) *The Body: The Key Concepts,* Oxford: Berg.

Bloomer, K. C., Moore, C. W. and Yudell, R. J. (1977) *Body, Memory and Architecture,* New Haven and London: Yale University Press.

Blundell Jones, P. and Meagher, M. (eds) (2015) *Architecture and Movement: The Dynamic Experience of Buildings and Landscapes*, New York: Routledge.

Borgmann, A. (1984) *Technology and the Character of Contemporary Life: A Philosophical Inquiry,* Chicago and London: University of Chicago Press.

Botvinick, M. and Cohen, J. (1998) 'Rubber hands "feel" touch that eyes see', *Nature,* 391(6669), p. 756.

Bourdieu, P. (1977) *Outline of a Theory of Practice,* trans. Nice, R. Cambridge: Cambridge University Press.

Bourdieu, P. (1990) *The Logic of Practice,* trans. Nice, R. Cambridge: Polity Press.

Bourdieu, P. (1998) *Practical Reason: On the Theory of Action,* Cambridge: Polity Press.

Braidotti, R. (2013) *The Posthuman,* Cambridge: Polity Press.

Brand, S. (1994) *How Buildings Learn: What Happens after They're Built,* New York and London: Viking.

Brandstetter, G. and Völckers, H. (eds) (2000) *Remembering the Body*, Ostfildern-Ruit: Hatje Cantz.

Bresler, L. (ed.) (2004) *Knowing Bodies, Moving Minds: Towards Embodied Teaching and Learning*, Dordrecht and London: Kluwer Academic.

Brook, P. (1976) *The Empty Space*, Harmondsworth: Penguin.

Bruner, J. S. (1990) *Acts of Meaning*, Cambridge, MA and London: Harvard University Press.

Bullivant, L. (2006) *Responsive Environments: Architecture, Art and Design*, London: V&A.

Burkitt, I. (1999) *Bodies of Thought: Embodiment, Identity and Modernity*, London: Sage.

Calvo-Merino, B., Grezes, J., Glaser, D. E., Passingham, R. E. and Haggard, P. (2006) 'Seeing or doing? Influence of visual and motor familiarity in action observation', *Current Biology,* 16(19), pp. 1905–1910.

Cannon, W. B. (1963) *The Wisdom of the Body,* New York: W. W. Norton.

Capra, F. (1996) *The Web of Life: A New Synthesis of Mind and Matter,* London: HarperCollins.

Caputo, J. D. (ed.) (1997) *Deconstruction in a Nutshell: A Conversation with Jacques Derrida*, New York: Fordham University Press.

Carman, T. (2008) *Merleau-Ponty,* London: Routledge.

Carman, T. and Hansen, M. B. N. (eds) (2005) *The Cambridge Companion to Merleau-Ponty*, Cambridge: Cambridge University Press.

Chemero, A. (2009) *Radical Embodied Cognitive Science,* Cambridge, MA and London: MIT Press.

Ching, F. D. K. (1996) *Architecture, Form, Space & Order,* 2nd edn. New York and Chichester: John Wiley.

Clark, A. (1997) *Being There: Putting Brain, Body, and World Together Again,* Cambridge, MA and London: MIT Press.

Clark, A. (2003) *Natural-Born Cyborgs: Why Minds and Technologies Are Made to Merge,* New York: Oxford University Press.

Clark, A. (2008) *Supersizing the Mind: Embodiment, Action, and Cognitive Extension,* New York and Oxford: Oxford University Press.

Clarke, B. and Hansen, M. B. N. (2009) *Emergence and Embodiment: New Essays on Second-Order Systems Theory,* Durham, NC and Chesham: Duke University Press.

Classen, C. (ed.) (2005) *The Book of Touch,* Oxford: Berg.

Colquhoun, A. (1969) 'Typology and design method', in Jencks, C. and Baird, G. (eds) *Meaning in Architecture,* New York: G. Braziller, pp. 267–277.

Coole, D. H. (2007) *Merleau-Ponty and Modern Politics after Anti-Humanism,* Lanham, MD and Plymouth: Rowman & Littlefield.

Coole, D. H. and Frost, S. (eds) (2010) *New Materialisms: Ontology, Agency, and Politics,* Durham, NC: Duke University Press.

Corballis, M. C. (2002) *From Hand to Mouth: The Origins of Language,* Princeton, NJ: Princeton University Press.

Crary, J. E. and Kwinter, S. E. (eds) (1992) *Incorporations,* New York: Zone Books.

Crossley, N. (2001) *The Social Body: Habit, Identity and Desire,* London: Sage.

Damasio, A. R. (2000) *The Feeling of What Happens: Body and Emotion in the Making of Consciousness,* London: Heinemann.

Damasio, A. R. (2005) *Descartes' Error: Emotion, Reason, and the Human Brain,* London: Penguin.

Damasio, A. R. (2010) *Self Comes to Mind: Constructing the Conscious Brain,* London: Heinemann.

Dawkins, R. (1999) *The Extended Phenotype: The Long Reach of the Gene,* Oxford: Oxford University Press.

De Certeau, M. (1984) *The Practice of Everyday Life,* trans. Rendall, S. Berkeley, CA and London: University of California Press.

Deacon, T. W. (1997) *The Symbolic Species: The Co-evolution of Language and the Brain,* New York and London: W.W. Norton.

Deleuze, G. and Guattari, F. (1988) *A Thousand Plateaus: Capitalism and Schizophrenia,* trans. Massumi, B. London: Athlone Press.

Dennett, D. C. (1992) *Consciousness Explained,* London: Penguin.

Descartes, R. (1985) *The Philosophical Writings of Descartes,* trans. Cottingham, J., Stoothoff, R. & Murdoch, D. Cambridge: Cambridge University Press.

Dewey, J. (1980) *Art as Experience* (originally published 1934), New York: Perigee Books.

Dillon, M. C. (ed.) (1991) *Merleau-Ponty Vivant*, Albany, NY: State University of New York Press.

Dillon, M. C. (1997) *Merleau-Ponty's Ontology,* 2nd edn. Evanston, IL: Northwestern University Press.

Diprose, R. and Reynolds, J. (2008) *Merleau-Ponty: Key Concepts,* Stocksfield: Acumen.

Donald, M. (1991) *Origins of the Modern Mind: Three Stages in the Evolution of Culture and Cognition,* Cambridge, MA and London: Harvard University Press.

Dourish, P. (2001) *Where the Action Is: The Foundations of Embodied Interaction,* Cambridge, MA: MIT Press.

Drake, S. (2005) 'The *Chiasm* and the experience of space', *Journal of Architectural Education,* 59(2), pp. 53–59.

Dudley, S. H. (ed.) (2010) *Museum Materialities: Objects, Engagements, Interpretations*, London: Routledge.

Edensor, T. (2005) *Industrial Ruins: Spaces, Aesthetics, and Materiality,* Oxford: Berg.

Eisenman, P., Krauss, R. E. and Tafuri, M. (1987) *House of Cards,* New York and Oxford: Oxford University Press.

Eliasson, O. (2013) *Your Embodied Garden.* Video, directed by Eliasson, O. Louisiana Museum, Denmark.

Feher, M., Naddaff, R. and Tazi, N. (eds) (1989) *Fragments for a History of the Human Body: Vol 1*, New York: Zone Books.

Flusser, V. (2014) *Gestures,* trans. Roth, N. A. Minneapolis: University of Minnesota Press.

Foster, H. (ed.) (1983) *The Anti-Aesthetic: Essays on Postmodern Culture*, Port Townsend, WA: Bay Press.

Foster, S. L. (2011) *Choreographing Empathy: Kinesthesia in Performance,* London: Routledge.

Foucault, M. (1994) *The Order of Things: An Archaeology of the Human Sciences,* New York: Vintage Books.

Frampton, K. (1983) 'Towards a Critical Regionalism: Six points for an architecture of resistance', in Foster, H. (ed.) *The Anti-Aesthetic: Essays on Postmodern Culture*, Port Townsend, WA: Bay Press, pp. 16–30.

Frampton, K. (1988) 'Intimations of tactility: Excerpts from a fragmentary polemic', in Marble, S. (ed.) *Architecture and Body*, New York: Rizzoli, unpaginated.

Frampton, K. (1990) '*Rappel a l'ordre*: The case for the tectonic', *Architectural Design,* 60(3–4), pp. 19–25.

Frampton, K. (1995) *Studies in Tectonic Culture: The Poetics of Construction in Nineteenth- and Twentieth-Century Architecture*. Edited by Cava, J. Cambridge, MA and London: MIT Press.

Frascari, M. (1984) 'The tell-the-tale detail', *VIA* (7: The Building of Architecture), pp. 23–37.

Frascari, M. (1990) *Monsters of Architecture: Anthropomorphism in Architectual Theory,* Totowa, NJ and London: Rowman & Littlefield.

Frascari, M. (2011) *Eleven Exercises in the Art of Architectural Drawing: Slow Food for the Architect's Imagination,* London: Routledge.

Frascari, M., Hale, J. and Starkey, B. (eds) (2007) *From Models to Drawings: Imagination and Representation in Architecture*, London: Routledge.

Freedberg, D. and Gallese, V. (2007) 'Motion, emotion and empathy in esthetic experience', *Trends in Cognitive Science,* 11(5), pp. 197–203.

Gallagher, S. (2005) *How the Body Shapes the Mind,* Oxford: Clarendon Press.

Gallagher, S. (2012) *Phenomenology,* Basingstoke: Palgrave Macmillan.

Gallagher, S. and Zahavi, D. (2008) *The Phenomenological Mind: An Introduction to Philosophy of Mind and Cognitive Science,* London: Routledge.

Gallese, V., Fadiga, L., Fogassi, L. and Rizzolatti, G. (1996) 'Action Recognition in the premotor cortex', *Brain,* 119 (2), pp. 593–609.

Gallese, V. and Goldman, A. (1998) 'Mirror Neurons and the Simulation Theory of Mind-Reading', *Trends in Cognitive Science,* 2(12), pp. 493–501.

Gibbs, R. W. (2005) *Embodiment and Cognitive Science,* Cambridge: Cambridge University Press.

Gibson, J. J. (1986) *The Ecological Approach to Visual Perception,* Hillsdale, NJ: Lawrence Erlbaum.

Gibson, K. R. and Ingold, T. (eds) (1993) *Tools, Language, and Cognition in Human Evolution*, Cambridge: Cambridge University Press.

Glendinning, S. (2006) *In the Name of Phenomenology,* London: Routledge.

Goldin-Meadow, S. (2003) *Hearing Gesture: How Our Hands Help Us Think,* Cambridge, MA and London: Belknap Press of Harvard University Press.

Goodale, M. A. and Milner, A. D. (2005) *Sight Unseen: An Exploration of Conscious and Unconscious Vision,* Oxford: Oxford University Press.

Gopnik, A., Meltzoff, A. N. and Kuhl, P. K. (2001) *How Babies Think: The Science of Childhood,* London: Phoenix.

Gregory, R. L. (1998) *Eye and Brain: The Psychology of Seeing,* 5th edn. Oxford: Oxford University Press.

Grosz, E. A. (1994) *Volatile Bodies: Toward a Corporeal Feminism,* Bloomington, IN: Indiana University Press.

Grosz, E. A. (1998) *Architecture from the Outside: Essays on Virtual and Real Space,* Cambridge, MA and London: MIT Press.

Hansell, M. H. (2007) *Built by Animals: The Natural History of Animal Architecture,* Oxford and New York: Oxford University Press.

Hansen, M. B. N. (2004) *New Philosophy for New Media,* Cambridge, MA and London: MIT Press.

Hansen, M. B. N. (2006) *Bodies in Code: Interfaces with Digital Media,* London: Routledge.

Hansen, M. F. (2003) *The Eloquence of Appropriation: Prolegomena to an Understanding of Spolia in Early Christian Rome,* Rome: L'Erma di Bretschneider.

Haraway, D. J. (1991) *Simians, Cyborgs and Women: The Reinvention of Nature,* London: Free Association.

Harman, G. (2011) *The Quadruple Object,* Winchester and Washington, DC: Zero Books.

Hass, L. (2008) *Merleau-Ponty's Philosophy,* Bloomington, IN: Indiana University Press.

Hauptmann, D. and Akkerhuis, B. (eds) (2006) *The Body in Architecture*, Rotterdam: 010.

Hayles, K. (1999) *How We Became Posthuman: Virtual Bodies in Cybernetics, Literature, and Informatics,* Chicago, IL and London: University of Chicago Press.

Heidegger, M. (1962) *Being and Time,* trans. Macquarrie, J. & Robinson, E. New York: HarperCollins.

Heidegger, M. (1977) *The Question Concerning Technology, and Other Essays,* trans. Lovitt, W. New York and London: Harper and Row.

Held, R. and Hein, A. (1963) 'Movement-produced stimulation in the development of visually guided behavior', *Journal of Comparative and Physiological Psychology,* 56, pp. 872–876.

Hensel, M., Hight, C. and Menges, A. (eds) (2009) *Space Reader: Heterogeneous Space in Architecture,* Chichester and Hoboken, NJ: Wiley.

Heschong, L. (1979) *Thermal Delight in Architecture,* Cambridge, MA and London: MIT Press.

Hill, J. (2003) *Actions of Architecture: Architects and Creative Users,* London and New York: Routledge.

Hill, J. (2012) *Weather Architecture,* London and New York: Routledge.

Holl, S. (1996) *Intertwining: Selected Projects 1989–1995,* New York: Princeton Architectural Press.

Holl, S. (2000) *Parallax,* Basel, Boston and New York: Birkhäuser and Princeton Architectural Press.

Holl, S., Pallasmaa, J. and Pérez-Gómez, A. (2006) *Questions of Perception: Phenomenology of Architecture,* 2nd edn. San Francisco, CA: William Stout.

Humphrey, N. (2006) *Seeing Red: A Study in Consciousness,* Cambridge, MA and London: Belknap Press of Harvard University Press.

Husserl, E. (1970) *The Crisis of European Sciences and Transcendental Phenomenology: An Introduction to Phenomenological Philosophy* (originally published 1936), trans. Carr, D. Evanston, IL: Northwestern University Press.

Husserl, E. (2001) *Logical Investigations, Vol. 1* (originally published 1900), trans. Findlay, J.N. London: Routledge.

Hutchins, E. (1995) *Cognition in the Wild,* Cambridge, MA and London: MIT Press.

Iacoboni, M. (2008) *Mirroring People: The New Science of How We Connect with Others,* New York: Farrar, Straus and Giroux.

Ihde, D. (1990) *Technology and the Lifeworld: From Garden to Earth,* Bloomington, IN: Indiana University Press.

Ihde, D. (2002) *Bodies in Technology,* Minneapolis and London: University of Minnesota Press.

Illich, I. (1985) *H$_2$O and the Waters of Forgetfulness: Reflections on the Historicity of "Stuff"*, Dallas: Dallas Institute of Humanities and Culture.

Ingold, T. (2000) *The Perception of the Environment: Essays on Livelihood, Dwelling and Skill,* London and New York: Routledge.

Ingold, T. (2013) *Making: Anthropology, Archaeology, Art and Architecture,* London and New York: Routledge.

Iriki, A. (2006) 'The neural origins and implications of imitation, mirror neurons and tool use', *Current Opinion in Neurobiology,* 16, pp. 660–667.

James, W. (1950) *The Principles of Psychology,* 2 vols (originally published 1890), New York: Dover.

Jameson, F. (1994) *The Seeds of Time,* New York and Chichester: Columbia University Press.

Jeannerod, M. (2006) *Motor Cognition: What Actions Tell the Self,* Oxford: Oxford University Press.

Johnson, G. A. and Smith, M. B. (eds) (1990) *Ontology and Alterity in Merleau-Ponty*, Evanston, IL: Northwestern University Press.

Johnson, G. A. and Smith, M. B. (eds) (1993) *The Merleau-Ponty Aesthetics Reader: Philosophy and Painting*, Evanston, IL: Northwestern University Press.

Johnson, M. (1987) *The Body in the Mind: The Bodily Basis of Meaning, Imagination, and Reason,* Chicago: University of Chicago Press.

Johnson, M. (2007) *The Meaning of the Body: Aesthetics of Human Understanding,* Chicago and London: University of Chicago Press.

Jones, C. A. and Arning, B. (2006) *Sensorium: Embodied Experience, Technology, and Contemporary Art,* Cambridge, MA and London: MIT Press.

Jullien, F. (1995) *The Propensity of Things: Toward a History of Efficacy in China,* trans. Lloyd, J. New York: Zone Books.

Katz, D. (1989) *The World of Touch,* trans. Krueger, L.E. Hillsdale, NJ: Lawrence Erlbaum Associates.

Kearney, R. (1994) *Modern Movements in European Philosophy,* Manchester: Manchester University Press.

Keller, C. M. and Keller, J. D. (1996) *Cognition and Tool Use: The Blacksmith at Work,* Cambridge: Cambridge University Press.

Kepes, G. (1995) *Language of Vision,* New York, Dover and London: Constable.

Kirsh, D. (1995) 'The intelligent use of space', *Artificial Intelligence,* 73(1–2), pp. 31–68.

Knappett, C. (2005) *Thinking through Material Culture: An Interdisciplinary Perspective,* Philadelphia: University of Pennsylvania Press.

Kockelmans, J. J. (1967) *Phenomenology: The Philosophy of Edmund Husserl and Its Interpretation,* Garden City, NY: Anchor Books.

Köhler, W. (1992) *Gestalt Psychology: An Introduction to New Concepts in Modern Psychology,* New York: Liveright.

Kozel, S. (2007) *Closer: Performance, Technologies, Phenomenology,* Cambridge, MA and London: MIT Press.

Krell, D. F. (1997) *Archeticture: Ecstasies of Space, Time, and the Human Body,* Albany, NY: State University of New York Press.

Kubler, G. (1962) *The Shape of Time: Remarks on the History of Things,* New Haven and London: Yale University Press.

Kuhn, T. S. (1970) *The Structure of Scientific Revolutions,* 2nd edn. Chicago and London: University of Chicago Press.

Lakoff, G. and Johnson, M. (1980) *Metaphors We Live By,* Chicago: University of Chicago Press.

Lakoff, G. and Johnson, M. (1999) *Philosophy in the Flesh: The Embodied Mind and Its Challenge to Western Thought,* New York: Basic Books.

Landes, D. A. (2013a) *Merleau-Ponty and the Paradoxes of Expression,* London and New York: Bloomsbury.

Landes, D. A. (2013b) *The Merleau-Ponty Dictionary,* London and New York: Bloomsbury.

Langer, M. M. (1989) *Merleau-Ponty's Phenomenology of Perception: A Guide and Commentary,* Gainesville, FL: Florida State University Press.

Latour, B. (1993) *We Have Never Been Modern,* trans. Porter, C. New York and London: Harvester Wheatsheaf.

Latour, B. (1999) *Pandora's Hope: Essays on the Reality of Science Studies,* Cambridge, MA and London: Harvard University Press.

Latour, B. (with Johnson, J.) (1988) 'Mixing humans and nonhumans together: The sociology of a door-closer', *Social Problems,* 35, pp. 298–310.

Lave, J. (1988) *Cognition in Practice: Mind, Mathematics and Culture in Everyday Life,* Cambridge: Cambridge University Press.

Lave, J. and Wenger, E. (1991) *Situated Learning: Legitimate Peripheral Participation,* Cambridge: Cambridge University Press.

Lavin, S. (1992) *Quatremère De Quincy and the Invention of a Modern Language of Architecture,* Cambridge, MA: MIT Press.

Le Corbusier, C. E. J. (1951) *The Modulor: A Harmonious Measure to the Human Scale Universally Applicable to Architecture and Mechanics,* London: Faber and Faber.

Le Corbusier, C. E. J. (2008) *Toward an Architecture,* trans. Goodman, J. London: Frances Lincoln.

Leach, N. (ed.) (1997) *Rethinking Architecture: A Reader in Cultural Theory*, London and New York: Routledge.

Leach, N., Turnbull, D. and Williams, C. (eds) (2004) *Digital Tectonics*, Chichester: Wiley-Academy.

Leatherbarrow, D. (2009) *Architecture Oriented Otherwise,* New York: Princeton Architectural Press.

Leatherbarrow, D. and Mostafavi, M. (2002) *Surface Architecture,* Cambridge, MA and London: MIT Press.

Leder, D. (1990) *The Absent Body,* Chicago: University of Chicago Press.

Lefaivre, L. and Tzonis, A. (2003) *Critical Regionalism: Architecture and Identity in a Globalized World,* Munich and London: Prestel.

Lefebvre, H. (1996) *Writings on Cities,* trans. Kofman, E. & Lebas, E. Oxford: Blackwell.

Lepecki, A. (2006) *Exhausting Dance: Performance and the Politics of Movement,* New York and London: Routledge.

Lepecki, A. (ed.) (2012) *Dance: Documents of Contemporary Art*, London and Cambridge, MA: Whitechapel Gallery, MIT Press.

Leroi-Gourhan, A. (1993) *Gesture and Speech,* trans. Berger, A.B. Cambridge, MA and London: MIT Press.

Lerup, L. (1977) *Building the Unfinished: Architecture and Human Action,* Beverly Hills and London: Sage.

Levin, D. M. (1985) *The Body's Recollection of Being: Phenomenological Psychology and the Deconstruction of Nihilism,* London: Routledge & Kegan Paul.

Lévi-Strauss, C. (1963) *Structural Anthropology,* trans. Jacobson, C. & Schoepf, B.G. New York: Basic Books.
Lévi-Strauss, C. (1966) *The Savage Mind,* Chicago and London: University of Chicago Press.
Lewis-Williams, J. D. (2004) *The Mind in the Cave: Consciousness and the Origins of Art,* London: Thames & Hudson.
Leyton, M. (2006) *Shape as Memory: A Geometric Theory of Architecture,* Basel: Birkhäuser.
Livingstone, M. S. (2002) *Vision and Art: The Biology of Seeing,* New York and London: Harry N. Abrams.
Long, R. (1991) *Walking in Circles,* London: South Bank Centre.
Lovelock, J. (1979) *Gaia: A New Look at Life on Earth,* Oxford: Oxford University Press.
Luria, A. R. (1982) *Language and Cognition,* trans. Wertsch, J. V. Washington, DC: Winston & Sons.
Lynch, K. (1960) *The Image of the City,* Cambridge MA and London: MIT Press.
Lynn, G. (1998) *Folds, Bodies & Blobs: Collected Essays,* Brussels: La Lettre volée.
Madison, G. B. (1981) *The Phenomenology of Merleau-Ponty: A Search for the Limits of Consciousness,* Athens, OH: Ohio University Press.
Maiese, M. (2011) *Embodiment, Emotion, and Cognition,* Basingstoke: Palgrave Macmillan.
Malafouris, L. (2013) *How Things Shape the Mind: A Theory of Material Engagement,* Cambridge, MA: MIT Press.
Malafouris, L. and Renfrew, C. (eds) (2010) *The Cognitive Life of Things: Recasting the Boundaries of the Mind*, Cambridge: McDonald Institute for Archaeological Research.
Mallgrave, H. F. (2010) *The Architect's Brain: Neuroscience, Creativity, and Architecture,* Chichester: Wiley-Blackwell.
Mallgrave, H. F. and Ikonomou, E. (eds) (1994) *Empathy, Form, and Space: Problems in German Aesthetics, 1873–1893*, Santa Monica, CA and Chicago, IL: Getty Center for the History of Art and the Humanities.
Malnar, J. M. and Vodvarka, F. (2004) *Sensory Design,* Minneapolis: University of Minnesota Press.
Marble, S. (ed.) (1988) *Architecture and Body*, New York: Rizzoli.

Marchand, T. H. J. (ed.) (2010) *Making Knowledge: Explorations of the Indissoluble Relation between Mind, Body and Environment*, Oxford: Wiley-Blackwell.

Marks, L. U. (2002) *Touch: Sensuous Theory and Multisensory Media*, Minneapolis: University of Minnesota Press.

Marras, A. (ed.) (1999) *Eco-Tec: Architecture of the in-Between*, New York: Princeton Architectural Press.

Massumi, B. (1998) 'Stelarc: The evolutionary alchemy of reason', in Beckmann, J. (ed.) *The Virtual Dimension: Architecture, Representation, and Crash Culture*, New York: Princeton Architectural Press, pp. 334–341.

Matthews, E. (2002) *The Philosophy of Merleau-Ponty*, Chesham: Acumen.

Maturana, H. R. and Varela, F. J. (1992) *The Tree of Knowledge: The Biological Roots of Human Understanding,* trans. Paolucci, R. 2nd edn. Boston and London: Shambhala.

Mauss, M. (2006) *Techniques, Technology and Civilisation,* trans. Schlanger, N. New York: Durkheim Press/Berghahn Books.

McCann, R. (2008) 'Entwining the body and the world: Architectural design and experience in the light of "eye and mind"', in Weiss, G. (ed.) *Intertwinings: Interdisciplinary Encounters with Merleau-Ponty*, Albany, NY: State University of New York Press, pp. 265–281.

McCarthy, J. and Wright, P. (2004) *Technology as Experience,* Cambridge, MA and London: MIT Press.

McCullough, M. (1996) *Abstracting Craft: The Practiced Digital Hand,* Cambridge, MA and London: MIT Press.

McCullough, M. (2004) *Digital Ground: Architecture, Pervasive Computing, and Environmental Knowing,* Cambridge, MA and London: MIT Press.

McLuhan, M. (2001) *Understanding Media: The Extensions of Man,* London: Routledge.

McManus, I. C. (2002) *Right Hand, Left Hand: The Origins of Asymmetry in Brains, Bodies, Atoms and Cultures,* London: Weidenfeld & Nicolson.

McNeill, D. (2005) *Gesture and Thought,* Chicago and London: University of Chicago Press.

McNeill, D. (1992) *Hand and Mind: What Gestures Reveal About Thought,* Chicago and London: University of Chicago Press.

Mead, G. H. and Morris, C. W. (1967) *Mind, Self and Society from the Standpoint of a Social Behaviorist,* Chicago: University of Chicago Press.

Menary, R. (ed.) (2010) *The Extended Mind*, Cambridge, MA and London: MIT Press.

Merleau-Ponty, M. (1962) *Phenomenology of Perception,* trans. Smith, C. London: Routledge & Kegan Paul.

Merleau-Ponty, M. (1963) *In Praise of Philosophy,* trans. Wild, J. & Edie, J. M. Evanston, IL: Northwestern University Press.

Merleau-Ponty, M. (1964a) *The Primacy of Perception, and Other Essays on Phenomenological Psychology, the Philosophy of Art, History, and Politics,* Evanston, IL: Northwestern University Press.

Merleau-Ponty, M. (1964b) *Sense and Non-Sense,* trans. Dreyfus, H.L. & Dreyfus, P.A. Evanston, IL: Northwestern University Press.

Merleau-Ponty, M. (1964c) *Signs,* trans. McCleary, R.C. Evanston, IL: Northwestern University Press.

Merleau-Ponty, M. (1968) *The Visible and the Invisible; Followed by Working Notes,* trans. Lingis, A. Evanston, IL: Northwestern University Press.

Merleau-Ponty, M. (1970) *Themes from the Lectures at the Collège de France, 1952–1960,* trans. O'Neill, J. Evanston, IL: Northwestern University Press.

Merleau-Ponty, M. (1973a) *Consciousness and the Acquisition of Language,* trans. Silverman, H.J. Evanston, IL: Northwestern University Press.

Merleau-Ponty, M. (1973b) *The Prose of the World,* trans. O'Neill, J. Evanston, IL: Northwestern University Press.

Merleau-Ponty, M. (1983) *The Structure of Behavior,* trans. Fisher, A.L. Pittsburgh, PA: Duquesne University Press.

Merleau-Ponty, M. (2003) *Nature: Course Notes from the Collège de France,* trans. Vallier, R. Evanston, IL: Northwestern University Press.

Merleau-Ponty, M. (2004) *The World of Perception,* trans. Davis, O. London: Routledge.

Merleau-Ponty, M. (2008) *The World of Perception,* trans. Davis, O. London: Routledge.

Merleau-Ponty, M. (2010) *Child Psychology and Pedagogy: The Sorbonne Lectures 1949–1952,* trans. Welsh, T. Evanston, IL: Northwestern University Press.

Merleau-Ponty, M. (2012) *Phenomenology of Perception,* trans. Landes, D.A. Abingdon and New York: Routledge.

Mindrup, M. (ed.) (2015) *The Material Imagination: Reveries on Architecture and Matter,* Farnham: Ashgate.

Mitcham, C. (1994) *Thinking through Technology: The Path between Engineering and Philosophy,* Chicago and London: University of Chicago Press.

Mithen, S. J. (1998) *The Prehistory of the Mind: A Search for the Origins of Art, Religion and Science,* London: Phoenix.

Moran, D. (2000) *Introduction to Phenomenology,* New York: Routledge.

Morris, D. (2004) *The Sense of Space,* Albany, NY: State University of New York Press.

Mostafavi, M. and Leatherbarrow, D. (1993) *On Weathering: The Life of Buildings in Time,* Cambridge, MA and London: MIT Press.

Mugerauer, R. (1995) *Interpreting Environments: Tradition, Deconstruction, Hermeneutics,* Austin, TX: University of Texas Press.

Nagel, T. (1979) *Mortal Questions,* London: Cambridge University Press.

Neisser, U. (1976) *Cognition and Reality: Principles and Implications of Cognitive Psychology,* San Francisco: W. H. Freeman.

Neutra, R. J. (1954) *Survival through Design,* New York: Oxford University Press.

Nochlin, L. (1994) *The Body in Pieces: The Fragment as a Metaphor of Modernity,* London: Thames and Hudson.

Noë, A. (2004) *Action in Perception,* Cambridge, MA and London: MIT Press.

Noë, A. (2009) *Out of Our Heads: Why You Are Not Your Brain, and Other Lessons from the Biology of Consciousness,* 1st edn. New York: Hill and Wang.

Noland, C. (2009) *Agency and Embodiment: Performing Gestures/Producing Culture,* Cambridge, MA: Harvard University Press.

Norberg-Schulz, C. (1966) *Intentions in Architecture,* Cambridge, MA: MIT Press.

Norberg-Schulz, C. (1971) *Existence, Space & Architecture,* London: Studio Vista.

Norberg-Schulz, C. (1985) *The Concept of Dwelling: On the Way to Figurative Architecture,* New York: Rizzoli.

Norman, D. A. (1993) *Things That Make Us Smart: Defending Human Attributes in the Age of the Machine,* Reading, MA: Addison-Wesley.

Olkowski, D. and Weiss, G. (eds) (2006) *Feminist Interpretations of Maurice Merleau-Ponty*, University Park, PA: Pennsylvania State University Press.

O'Neill, J. (1970) *Perception, Expression, and History; The Social Phenomenology of Maurice Merleau-Ponty,* Evanston, IL: Northwestern University Press.

O'Neill, J. (1989) *The Communicative Body: Studies in Communicative Philosophy, Politics, and Sociology,* Evanston, IL: Northwestern University Press.

Ong, W. J. (1991) *Orality and Literacy: The Technologizing of the Word*, London and New York: Routledge.

Oosterhuis, K. (2003) *Hyperbodies: Toward an E-Motive Architecture*, Basel and Boston: Birkhäuser.

Otero-Pailos, J. (2010) *Architecture's Historical Turn: Phenomenology and the Rise of the Postmodern,* Minneapolis: University of Minnesota Press.

Pallasmaa, J. (2005) *The Eyes of the Skin: Architecture and the Senses,* Chichester: Wiley-Academy.

Pallasmaa, J. (2009) *The Thinking Hand: Existential and Embodied Wisdom in Architecture,* Chichester and Hoboken, NJ: Wiley.

Pascoe, D. (1997) *Peter Greenaway: Museums and Moving Images,* London: Reaktion.

Paterson, M. (2007) *The Senses of Touch: Haptics, Affects and Technologies,* Oxford and New York: Berg.

Perec, G. (1997) *Species of Spaces and Other Pieces,* trans. Sturrock, J. London: Penguin.

Pérez-Gómez, A. (1983) *Architecture and the Crisis of Modern Science,* Cambridge, MA: MIT Press.

Pérez-Gómez, A. (1986) 'The renovation of the body', *AA Files,* (13), pp. 26–29.

Pfeifer, R., Bongard, J. and Grand, S. (2007) *How the Body Shapes the Way We Think: A New View of Intelligence,* Cambridge, MA and London: MIT Press.

Piaget, J. and Inhelder, B. (1956) *The Child's Conception of Space,* trans. Langdon, F. J. & Lunzer, J. L. London: Routledge & Kegan Paul.

Pickering, A. (1995) *The Mangle of Practice: Time, Agency, and Science,* Chicago and London: University of Chicago Press.

Pickering, A. and Guzik, K. (eds) (2008) *The Mangle in Practice: Science, Society, and Becoming*, Durham, NC and London: Duke University Press.

Picon, A. and Ponte, A. (eds) (2003) *Architecture and the Sciences: Exchanging Metaphors*, New York: Princeton Architectural Press.

Pink, S. (2011) 'From embodiment to emplacement: Re-thinking competing bodies, senses and spatialities', *Sport, Education and Society,* 16(3), pp. 343–355.

Plato (1973) *The Collected Dialogues of Plato: Including the Letters,* trans. Hamilton, E. & Cairns, H. Princeton, NJ: Princeton University Press.

Polanyi, M. (1958) *Personal Knowledge; Towards a Post-Critical Philosophy,* Chicago: University of Chicago Press.

Porter, R. (2003) *Flesh in the Age of Reason,* London: Allen Lane.

Postman, N. (1993) *Technopoly: The Surrender of Culture to Technology,* New York: Vintage.

Potts, A. (2000) *The Sculptural Imagination: Figurative, Modernist, Minimalist,* New Haven and London: Yale University Press.

Priest, S. (2003) *Merleau-Ponty,* London: Routledge.

Prigogine, I. and Stengers, I. (1985) *Order out of Chaos: Man's New Dialogue with Nature,* London: Flamingo.

Prinz, J. J. (2004) *Gut Reactions: A Perceptual Theory of Emotion*, Oxford and New York: Oxford University Press.

Prinz, J. J. (2012) *Beyond Human Nature: How Culture and Experience Shape the Human Mind,* New York: W.W. Norton.

Proudfoot, M. (ed.) (2003) *The Philosophy of Body*, Oxford: Blackwell.

Pylyshyn, Z. W. (2007) *Things and Places: How the Mind Connects with the World,* Cambridge, MA and London: MIT Press.

Rajchman, J. (1998) *Constructions,* Cambridge, MA and London: MIT Press.

Ramachandran, V. S. (2003) *The Emerging Mind: The Reith Lectures 2003,* London: Profile.

Ramachandran, V. S. (2013) 'The neurons that shaped civilization', [video lecture] in *Being Human* [online]. Available at: http://www.beinghuman.org/article/v-s-ramachandran-gandhi-neurons (accessed 8 July, 2015).

Ramachandran, V. S. and Blakeslee, S. (1998) *Phantoms in the Brain: Human Nature and the Architecture of the Mind,* London: Fourth Estate.

Renfrew, C., Frith, C. D. and Malafouris, L. (eds) (2009) *The Sapient Mind: Archaeology Meets Neuroscience*, Oxford: Oxford University Press.

Renfrew, C. and Morley, I. (eds) (2009) *Becoming Human: Innovation in Prehistoric Material and Spiritual Culture*, Cambridge: Cambridge University Press.

Ricoeur, P. (1981) *Hermeneutics and the Human Sciences: Essays on Language, Action and Interpretation,* trans. Thompson, J. B. Cambridge: Cambridge University Press.

Rizzolatti, G. and Sinigaglia, C. (2008) *Mirrors in the Brain: How Our Minds Share Actions and Emotions,* trans. Anderson, F. Oxford: Oxford University Press.

Roelstraete, D. (2010) *Richard Long: A Line Made by Walking,* London: Afterall Books.

Romdenh-Romluc, K. (2011) *Merleau-Ponty and Phenomenology of Perception,* London: Routledge.

Rose, S. P. R. (2003) *The Making of Memory: From Molecules to Mind,* 2nd edn. London: Vintage.

Rossi, A. (1982) *The Architecture of the City,* trans. Ghirardo, D. & Ockman, J. Cambridge, MA and London: MIT Press.

Rowe, C. and Koetter, F. (1978) *Collage City,* Cambridge, MA: MIT Press.

Rowlands, M. (2006) *Body Language: Representation in Action,* Cambridge, MA and London: MIT Press.

Rowlands, M. (2010) *The New Science of the Mind: From Extended Mind to Embodied Phenomenology,* Cambridge, MA and London: MIT Press.

Rush, F. L. (2009) *On Architecture: Thinking in Action*, London: Routledge.

Ryker, L. (ed.) (1995) *Mockbee Coker: Thought and Process*, New York: Princeton Architectural Press.

Rykwert, J. (1981) *On Adam's House in Paradise: The Idea of the Primitive Hut in Architectural History,* 2nd edn. Cambridge, MA: MIT Press.

Rykwert, J. (1996) *The Dancing Column: On Order in Architecture,* Cambridge, MA and London: MIT Press.

Rykwert, J., Dodds, G. and Tavernor, R. (eds) (2002) *Body and Building: Essays on the Changing Relation of Body and Architecture*, Cambridge, MA and London: MIT Press.

Ryle, G. (1963) *The Concept of Mind* (originally published 1949), London: Penguin Books.
Sacks, O. W. (2007) *The Man Who Mistook His Wife for a Hat,* London: Picador.
Scarry, E. (1985) *The Body in Pain: The Making and Unmaking of the World,* New York and Oxford: Oxford University Press.
Schechner, R. (1994) *Environmental Theater,* expanded 2nd edn. New York and London: Applause.
Schilder, P. F. (1935) *The Image and Appearance of the Human Body: Studies in the Constructive Energies of the Psyche,* London: Kegan Paul.
Schön, D. A. (1991) *The Reflective Practitioner: How Professionals Think in Action,* Aldershot: Avebury.
Schutz, A. (1967) *The Phenomenology of the Social World,* trans. Walsh, G. & Lehnert, F. Evanston, IL: Northwestern University Press.
Scott, F. (2008) *On Altering Architecture,* London: Routledge.
Searle, J. R. (1995) *The Construction of Social Reality,* London: Allen Lane.
Semper, G. (1989) *The Four Elements of Architecture and Other Writings, Res Monographs in Anthropology and Aesthetics,* trans. Mallgrave, H. F. & Herrmann, W. Cambridge: Cambridge University Press.
Sennett, R. (1994) *Flesh and Stone: The Body and the City in Western Civilization,* London: Faber.
Serota, N. (1996) *Experience or Interpretation: The Dilemma of Museums of Modern Art,* London: Thames and Hudson.
Shapiro, L. A. (2011) *Embodied Cognition,* London: Routledge.
Sharr, A. (2007) *Heidegger for Architects,* Abingdon and New York: Routledge.
Sheets-Johnstone, M. (2009) *The Corporeal Turn: An Interdisciplinary Reader,* Exeter: Imprint Academic.
Sheets-Johnstone, M. (2011) *The Primacy of Movement,* expanded 2nd edn. Amsterdam and Philadelphia: John Benjamins.
Shilling, C. (2003) *The Body and Social Theory,* 2nd edn. London: Sage.
Shusterman, R. (2008) *Body Consciousness: A Philosophy of Mindfulness and Somaesthetics,* Cambridge: Cambridge University Press.
Shusterman, R. (2012) *Thinking through the Body: Essays in Somaesthetics,* Cambridge and New York: Cambridge University Press.

Silverman, H. J. (1997) *Inscriptions: After Phenomenology and Structuralism,* Evanston, IL: Northwestern University Press.

Smith, M. and Morra, J. (eds) (2006) *The Prosthetic Impulse: From a Posthuman Present to a Biocultural Future,* Cambridge, MA and London: MIT Press.

Sobchack, V. C. (1992) *The Address of the Eye: A Phenomenology of Film Experience,* Princeton, NJ and Oxford: Princeton University Press.

Sobchack, V. C. (2004) *Carnal Thoughts: Embodiment and Moving Image Culture,* Berkeley, CA and London: University of California Press.

Spuybroek, L. (2004) *Nox: Machining Architecture,* London: Thames & Hudson.

Stafford, B. M. (1991) *Body Criticism: Imaging the Unseen in Enlightenment Art and Medicine,* Cambridge, MA and London: MIT Press.

Steadman, P. (2008) *The Evolution of Designs: Biological Analogy in Architecture and the Applied Arts,* 2nd edn. London: Routledge.

Stern, D. N. (2004) *The Present Moment in Psychotherapy and Everyday Life,* New York: W. W. Norton.

Stiegler, B. (1998) *Technics and Time: The Fault of Epimetheus,* trans. Beardsworth, R. & Collins, G. Stanford, CA: Stanford University Press.

Stockwell, P. (2002) *Cognitive Poetics: An Introduction,* London: Routledge.

Suchman, L. A. (2007) *Human-Machine Reconfigurations: Plans and Situated Actions,* 2nd edn. Cambridge: Cambridge University Press.

Tallis, R. (2003) *The Hand: A Philosophical Inquiry into Human Being,* Edinburgh: Edinburgh University Press.

Taylor, T. J. (2010) *The Artificial Ape: How Technology Changed the Course of Human Evolution,* New York: Palgrave Macmillan.

Thrift, N. J. (1996) *Spatial Formations,* London: Sage.

Tilley, C. Y. (1994) *A Phenomenology of Landscape: Places, Paths, and Monuments,* Oxford and Providence, RI: Berg.

Tilley, C. Y. and Bennett, W. (2004) *The Materiality of Stone: Explorations in Landscape Phenomenology,* Oxford: Berg.

Todes, S. (2001) *Body and World,* 2nd edn. Cambridge, MA and London: MIT Press.

Tomasello, M. (1999) *The Cultural Origins of Human Cognition,* Cambridge, MA: Harvard University Press.

Tomasello, M. (2005) *Constructing a Language: A Usage-Based Theory of Language Acquisition,* Cambridge, MA and London: Harvard University Press.

Tschumi, B. (1994) *Architecture and Disjunction,* Cambridge, MA and London: MIT Press.

Tufnell, M. and Crickmay, C. (1990) *Body, Space, Image: Notes Towards Improvisation and Performance,* London: Virago.

Turner, B. S. (2008) *The Body & Society: Explorations in Social Theory,* 3rd edn. London: Sage.

Turner, J. S. (2000) *The Extended Organism: The Physiology of Animal-Built Structures,* Cambridge, MA and London: Harvard University Press.

Turner, V. W. (1982) *From Ritual to Theatre: The Human Seriousness of Play,* New York: Performing Arts Journal Publications.

Turrell, J., Birnbaum, D. and Noever, P. (eds) (1999) *James Turrell: The Other Horizon,* Ostfildern-Ruit and New York: Hatje Cantz.

Uexküll, J. von (2010) *A Foray into the Worlds of Animals and Humans: With a Theory of Meaning,* trans. O'Neill, J. D. Minneapolis: University of Minnesota Press.

Van Berkel, B. (1999) 'A day in the life: Mobius House by Un Studio/Van Berkel & Bos', *Building Design,* (1385), pp. 15–16.

Van Schaik, L. (2008) *Spatial Intelligence: New Futures for Architecture,* Chichester and Hoboken, NJ: Wiley.

Varela, F. J. (1999) *Ethical Know-How: Action, Wisdom, and Cognition,* Stanford, CA: Stanford University Press.

Varela, F. J., Thompson, E. and Rosch, E. (1991) *The Embodied Mind: Cognitive Science and Human Experience,* Cambridge, MA and London: MIT Press.

Venturi, R. (1977) *Complexity and Contradiction in Architecture,* 2nd edn. London: Architectural Press.

Vesely, D. (2004) *Architecture in the Age of Divided Representation: The Question of Creativity in the Shadow of Production,* Cambridge, MA and London: MIT Press.

Vico, G. (1984) *The New Science of Giambattista Vico, Cornell Paperbacks,* trans. Bergin, T. G. & Fisch, M. H. Ithaca, NY: Cornell University Press.

Vidler, A. (2000) *Warped Space: Art, Architecture, and Anxiety in Modern Culture,* Cambridge, MA and London: MIT Press.

Vygotsky, L. S. (1986) *Thought and Language,* trans. Kozulin, A. Cambridge, MA: MIT Press.

Weinstock, M. (2010) *The Architecture of Emergence: The Evolution of Form in Nature and Civilisation,* Chichester: Wiley.

Weiss, G. (1999) *Body Images: Embodiment as Intercorporeality,* New York and London: Routledge.

Weiss, G. (ed.) (2008a) *Intertwinings: Interdisciplinary Encounters with Merleau-Ponty*, Albany, NY: State University of New York Press.

Weiss, G. (2008b) *Refiguring the Ordinary,* Bloomington, IN: Indiana University Press.

Welton, D. (ed.) (1998) *Body and Flesh: A Philosophical Reader*, Malden, MA: Blackwell.

Welton, D. (ed.) (1999) *The Body: Classic and Contemporary Readings*, Malden, MA: Blackwell.

Wenger, E. (1998) *Communities of Practice: Learning, Meaning, and Identity,* Cambridge: Cambridge University Press.

Weston, R. (2003) *Materials, Form and Architecture,* London: Laurence King.

Wheeler, M. (2005) *Reconstructing the Cognitive World: The Next Step,* Cambridge, MA and London: MIT Press.

Whitehead, A. N. (2004) *The Concept of Nature: The Tarner Lectures Delivered in Trinity College, November 1919,* Mineola, NY: Dover.

Wiener, N. (1961) *Cybernetics: Or Control and Communication in the Animal and the Machine,* trans. Oberli-Turner, M. & Schelbert, C. 2nd edn. Cambridge, MA: MIT Press.

Wigley, M. (1993) *The Architecture of Deconstruction: Derrida's Haunt,* Cambridge, MA: MIT Press.

Wilson, F. R. (1998) *The Hand: How Its Use Shapes the Brain, Language, and Human Culture,* New York: Pantheon.

Wolf, M. and Stoodley, C. J. (2008) *Proust and the Squid: The Story and Science of the Reading Brain,* Thriplow: Icon.

Wölfflin, H. (1994) 'Prolegomena to a psychology of architecture', in Vischer, R., Mallgrave, H.F. and Ikonomou, E. (eds) *Empathy, Form, and Space: Problems in German Aesthetics, 1873–1893*, Santa Monica, CA: Getty Center for the History of Art and the Humanities, pp. 150–190.

Yates, F. A. (1992) *The Art of Memory,* London: Pimlico.

Yeang, K. (1999) *The Green Skyscraper: The Basis for Designing Sustainable Intensive Buildings,* Munich and London: Prestel.

Young, I. M. (1980) 'Throwing like a girl: A phenomenology of feminine body comportment, motility and spatiality', *Human Studies,* 3(2), pp. 137–156.

Young, I. M. (1990) *Throwing Like a Girl and Other Essays in Feminist Philosophy and Social Theory,* Bloomington, IN: Indiana University Press.

Zaner, R. M. (1964) *The Problem of Embodiment. Some Contributions to a Phenomenology of the Body,* The Hague: Martinus Nijhoff.

Zumthor, P. (2006) *Thinking Architecture,* trans. Oberli-Turner, M. & Schelbert, C. 2nd edn. Basel and Boston: Birkhäuser.

# Index

actor-network theory 65, 84
adaptive re-use 23, 108
aesthetics 2, 5, 54–5
affordances 18, 22, 26, 78, 83, 89, 92–3, 106
Aristotle 56
Arnheim, Rudolf 59
atmosphere 53, 77, 86, 105

Bach-y-Rita, Paul 41
Barbaras, Renaud 64
Barthes, Roland 107
Beauvoir, Simone de 6, 7
Bennett – *Vibrant Matter* 83
Berthoz, Alain 60–1
bodily cognition 29
bodily exploration 47
body schemas 13–17, 24, 29, 90
boundary 30, 34, 66
Bourdieu, Pierre 24–5, 90
*bricolage* 99
building types 98

CAD 103
Campanella, Tommaso 53
Caruso St John Architects 79–81
Chalmers, David 35
chiasm 68, 76
Clark, Andy 34–5, 90

climate (weathering) 4, 76, 107
cognition 36
'coherent deformation' 25, 27, 95, 98, 99, 104
Collège de France 27, 63
*contrapposto* 56
critical functionalism 22
Critical Regionalism 99, 110
cyborg 84

Damasio, Antonio 21
dance 88, 102
Deleuze, Gilles 65
Derrida, Jacques 8, 65, 100
Dewey, John 26–7, 30, 75
drawing instruments 105
Dreyfus, Hubert 32
dwelling 4, 114

Eisenman, Peter 22–3, 105
Eliasson, Olafur 47
embodiment 6, 38
emergence 7, 9–10, 36–7, 38, 68, 96, 101
empathy 54–6, 113–14
epistemology 64
ethics 5, 82
evolution 25, 38, 102
experiential blindness 43

experiential learning 110
Eyck, Aldo van 78

fight or flight response 51
flesh (of the world) 65, 83, 112
Fontana, Lucio 72
Foucault, Michel 8, 109
found spaces 108
Frampton, Kenneth 4, 75, 99, 109–10
Frascari, Marco 75–6, 105
Freedberg, David 72
functional expression 22

Gaia theory *see* Lovelock, James
Gallagher, Shaun 36
Gallese, Vittorio 50
Gehry, Frank 107
Gestalt psychology 4, 38, 59
Graves, Michael 59
Grosz, Elizabeth 6
'gut reactions' 52, 91

habit 33
habitus 24
Haraway, Donna 84
Harman, Graham 70, 93
Heidegger, Martin 1, 3, 4, 11, 23, 28, 34, 59; *Being and Time* 4, 28–9
Held and Hein 42–3
Hertzberger, Herman 78
Holl, Steven 4, 48, 55, 67
horizontal structure 44–5, 46
House VI *see* Eisenman, Peter

Humphrey, Nicholas 69–70
Husserl, Edmund 3

Ingold, Tim 106
inhabitation 33
intentionality 63
interior design 22, 35

James, William 53, 65

Kahn, Louis 74, 75, 82

Lacan, Jacques 71
Landes, Donald 89
language 74, 97, 100–1, 104, 107, 111, 113; evolution of 25–7, 102; of architecture 55; of experience 90–6
Latour, Bruno 65, 105
Le Corbusier 59
Leatherbarrow, David 55–6
Lerup, Lars 77
*Les Temps Modernes* 7
Lévi-Strauss, Claude 26
Lewis Glucksman Gallery, Cork *see* O'Donnell + Tuomey
Locke, John 40
Long, Richard 72–3
Lovelock, James 84

Madison, Gary Brent 64, 116
Mallgrave, Harry Francis 72
Malraux, André 95

materiality 4, 67, 79, 82, 95, 100, 105–6, 109, 113–14; and embodiment 38; and perceptibility 13, 66; and tectonics 74–5; of language 107
Matisse, Henri 102
Maturana and Varela 89
Mauss, Marcel 49
memory 20–22
mind-body dualism 11, 64, 65
mirror neurons 50–1, 90
mirror stage 71
Molyneux, William 40
Moore, Charles 59
Morris, David 32
motor cognition 16–17, 19–20, 78, 88
motor echo 53
museum 45, 86, 93, 107
music 42

New Art Gallery, Walsall 79–81
Noland, Carrie 109
Norberg-Schulz, Christian 4

O'Donnell + Tuomey 55, 57
'On the Phenomenology of Language' 24, 92–3
O'Neill, John 93
ontogenesis/ontogenetic 38, 49, 68
optical illusion 39, 47

Pallasmaa, Juhani 27
perspective 46, 48, 108

phenomenology 1, 2–5, 9–11, 23, 59, 87
*Phenomenology of Perception* 4, 7, 11, 14, 63, 64, 68, 101
physiognomy 50, 53, 54, 113
place 18, 20
place, spirit of 4
Pollock, Jackson 72
posthumanism 2, 34, 66, 84
Potts, Alex – *The Sculptural Imagination* 74
Prinz, Jesse 52
proprioception 14–15, 40, 42–3

Ramachandran, V. S. 50
retentions and protentions (Husserl) 43, 46
reversibility 52–3, 112–13
Ricoeur, Paul 78, 82
Rossi, Aldo 98–9
Rowe, Colin 98–9
Rykwert, Joseph 58
Ryle, Gilbert 19

Sartre, Jean-Paul 7, 23
Saussure, Ferdinand de 26, 100–1
Scarpa. Carlo 75
Scharoun, Hans 48
scholar gardens 47
Schön, Donald 76
Scott, Fred – *On Altering Architecture* 108
sea squirt 38
Semper, Gottfried 99

sensory substitution 41
*shi* 83
simulation theory 53
solicitations of the world 17, 24, 44, 48, 89
space 1, 4, 18, 27–8, 37, 40, 42–3, 46–8, 66, 70, 78, 89, 103, 107; and body schema 16, 19; and embodiment 12, 14, 32–3, 113; found 108; function of 22; meaning of 83
Spatial Agency 78, 99
'speaking and spoken speech' 94–5
spirit of place 4
Stelarc – Third Hand 30–1
Stratton, George Malcolm 40–1
stream of consciousness 102
*Structure of Behavior, The* 7, 18, 28
Suzhou 47
synaesthesia 39

technology 34, 35–6, 49, 66–7, 76
tectonics 74–5
'theory of truth' 63

Turrell, James 47
typology 98, 106

Uexküll, Jakob von 2, 27, 28
*Umwelt* 2, 90
universal harmony 59, 60
universal space 22

Vico, Giambattista 56
Viola, Bill 109
*Visible and the Invisible, The* 8, 64, 67
vitalism 84
Vitruvius 58

weathering *see climate*
Weiss, Gail 96–7
Wertheimer, Max 41

Yeang, Ken – *The Green Skyscraper* 85
Young, Marion 6

Zumthor, Peter 4, 105